TOKYO MUSEUMS

A Complete Guide

Thomas and Ellen Flannigan

TOKYO
MUSEUMS

A Complete Guide

東京の博物館

Charles E. Tuttle Company
Rutland, Vermont & Tokyo, Japan

To our fathers, who introduced us
to the world of museums.

Special thanks to Ralph Frary,
without whose help this book could not have been completed.

Published by the Charles E. Tuttle Company, Inc.
of Rutland, Vermont & Tokyo, Japan
with editorial offices at
2-6 Suido 1-chome, Bunkyo-ku, Tokyo 112

© 1993 by Charles E. Tuttle Publishing Co., Inc.

LCC Card No. 93-60061
ISBN 0-8048-1892-4
First edition, 1993

Printed in Japan

CONTENTS

HISTORY 99

INTRODUCTION

When we came to live in Tokyo in February, 1991, we immediately started the difficult process of finding an apartment. Our fear of the next big Tokyo earthquake made it imperative to learn about which areas in Tokyo were the most dangerous. Our second day was one of Japan's many national holidays, so we decided to head to an obscure destination: the Kanto Earthquake Museum in Sumida Ward.

We wandered the halls of this deserted, haunting museum, thinking about the past and future. Suddenly, we had an idea: writing a book about Tokyo's Museums. We started the day looking for fault lines; we ended it talking about writing a book.

At first, it seemed like an impractical idea. How could we find enough time to travel around Tokyo while working at law firms? However, the more we journeyed out on the weekends and found odd neighborhoods harboring even odder museums, the more we liked the idea. We began rummaging through newspapers and magazines to find more museums. We became devoted to NHK's program on Sunday nights that covered the museum beat. By the time the rainy season arrived, the project was in full flower.

We have tried to produce a book that does more than tell you where the museums are and what they have on the shelves. The book is opinionated. We hope it makes you think.

ARCHAEOLOGY

考古学

Ancient Oriental Museum

*Yamanote Line or Marunouchi Line to Ikebukuro Station.
Ten-minute walk.*

This museum, founded in 1973, is particularly strong in Syrian archaeology. The museum has sponsored several expeditions to Syria to bring back many priceless artifacts. The brochure explains that museum curators were invited to northern Syria by UNESCO to fetch artifacts threatened by waters advancing from a dam on the Euphrates River.

There are video displays in the lobby, and there is a mock-up of Palmyra in the main hall. The short video showing Palmyra alone justifies a visit. A slide show in the center of the museum depicts the crucial excavations that produced the museum's collection.

The Ancient Oriental Museum is located in teeming Ikebukuro, on the seventh floor of the Bunka Kaikan, in the vast Sunshine City complex. If you come here on the weekend, make sure you have the patience and time to explore. The crowds on the way are intense.

Sunshine City also has a planetarium and an aquarium. If you would like to visit these museums as well as the Oriental Museum, there is a budget ticket valid for all three at a discounted price.

Kodai Oriento Hakubutsukan
3-1-4 Higashi-Ikebukuro, Toshima-ku, Tokyo
Tel: 3989-3491

Hours: 10:00–5:00.
Closed Monday.

Admission: ¥800,
¥400 for students.

Kokugakuin University Archaeological Museum

Bus #3 from Shibuya Station to Kokugakuin Daigakumae.
One-minute walk. See Map 4.

Tokyo is thick with archaeology museums, most of them long on presentation but short on collection. This one, planted in the picturesque campus of Kokugakuin University, is just the opposite. You could hardly cram more priceless artifacts into the small museum which could triple in floor space and still not do justice to the collection.

Artifacts from the Jomon and Kamakura eras abound, but the museum does not stop there. The Korean and Chinese items are just as impressive; virtually all of the everyday items from medieval villages in these countries are stuck somewhere in a nook of this museum.

The Kokugakuin University campus is a nice place to stroll, with many museums in its environs. It is amazing how peaceful it seems, with Shibuya just over the horizon.

Kokugakuin Daigaku Kokogaku Shiryokan
4-10-28 Higashi, Shibuya-ku, Tokyo
Tel: 5466-0249

Hours: 9:00–5:00.
Closed Sunday.   Admission: Free.

Meiji University Archaeological Museum

Hanzomon or Shinjuku Line to Jinbocho Station. Ten-minute walk.
See Map 1.

This museum is one of three museums located in the same building at Meiji University. It is part of the University archaeology department and displays the best pieces unearthed at various digs over the years. The displays are colorful and informative. All have impeccable English translations.

Visitors will be surprised to see the remains of Japanese elephants and other prehistoric creatures. Such creatures were gradually displaced by prehistoric settlers, who are represented not only by artists' conceptions, but also by remarkably advanced pottery.

The collection is heavily weighted towards Japanese archaeology, but there are a few displays of Meiji University excavations in foreign countries. Anyone with an ounce of curiosity will enjoy this museum, and the price is right.

Meiji Daigaku Kokogaku Hakubutsukan
1-1 Kanda Surugadai, Chiyoda-ku, Tokyo
Tel: 3296-4432

Hours: 10:00–4:30.
10:00–12:30, Saturday.
Closed Sunday.   Admission: Free.

Shirane Memorial Museum

Shibuya Station East Exit, bus #3 to Kokugakuin Daigakumae.
See Map 4.

This museum is located in the house of Zenchu Shirane, a politician who lived in the area around Kokugakuin University for much of his life. The house has a small but good collection of artifacts from the Jomon and Yayoi eras. Some of the pottery and tools may be three thousand years old.

One of the most interesting displays is a collection of photographs showing replicas of ancient Japanese houses from the Jomon era. The houses resemble Mongolian yurts or the tepees built by native American tribes.

The curator of the Shirane Museum aims to please. He was so excited to get foreign visitors that he provided an energetic tour of the museum and the surrounding neighborhood. The museum is located on the edge of the Kokugakuin University campus, so it is easy to combine a visit to this museum with a visit to Kokugakuin University's Shinto Museum and Archaeology Museum. Visitors on a Saturday morning may be treated to an outdoor Shinto wedding, with strange traditional music wafting through the campus.

Shirane Kinen Kyodo Bunkakan
4-9-1 Higashi, Shibuya-ku, Tokyo
Tel: 3407-8615

Hours: 9:00–5:00.
Closed Monday.   Admission: Free.

19

Yuasa Memorial Museum

Chuo Line to Mitaka Station. ICU bus to campus of International Christian University. Five-minute walk.

Hachiro Yuasa was born in Japan, but went to the US to study at the University of Illinois. He returned to earn a doctorate at Tokyo University. Yuasa was fired from his job in 1937 for his pacifist views, and spent the war years in the US. He was instrumental in obtaining permission from Japanese industrialists to allow Protestant missionaries to establish a university in suburban Tokyo.

The museum occupies a tranquil corner of one of the most beautifully landscaped universities on the planet. It is in a new building with glass walls facing one of the lovely ICU gardens. The first floor is devoted to folk consumes from Japan.

The best place to spend your time is the second floor. Here, you can find a sizable collection of relics from the Japanese Jomon period, the era shortly after the birth of Christ and before recorded accounts of contact with other nations. The amazing thing about this collection is that most of the artifacts were found within walking distance of the museum. When the foundations were being laid for the buildings, the excavations yielded a bonanza of remnants of the early Japanese who dwelled in the area.

Yuasa Hachiro Kinenkan
3-10-2 Osawa, Mitaka-shi, Tokyo
Tel: 0422-33-3340

Hours: 10:00–5:00.
10:00–4:30, Saturday.
Closed Sunday and Monday.

Admission: Free.

ARCHITECTURE

建築

Otani Museum of Art

Namboku Line to Nishigahara Station, Exit 2. Six-minute walk.

Located in Furukawa Park, this Renaissance-style stone home is beautiful on the outside but barren on the inside. The building was designed by the famous architect Dr. Jonah Conder, who also designed the Nikolai Cathedral in Tokyo. It resembles the home of an English nobleman and consists of natural slates and bricks.

You have to pay ¥100 just to see the outside of the home, but if you go in summer the rose garden justifies the admission price. The other gardens include ponds, a waterfall, and steep bluffs. The grounds seem particularly popular with young couples; many meander around the walks, furtively holding hands and looking at the flowers.

Otani Bijutsukan
1-27-39 Nishigahara, Kita-ku, Tokyo
Tel: 3910-0394

Hours: 9:30–4:30.
Closed Monday.
Appointment necessary.   Admission: ¥100.

Tokyo Metropolitan Teien Museum

*Yamanote Line to Meguro Station, East Exit. Seven-minute walk.
See Map 3.*

When the Tokyo City Government is the sponsor of a museum, you can generally be sure that it will be opulent and rich. This is the opposite of the situation in much of the world where civic museums are literally falling apart. At least some of Japan's spectacular wealth is being used for a good purpose.

The Teien Art Museum was completed in 1933. The building was designed by Henri Rapin, the French art-deco designer. The building served as the residence of Prince Asaka who lived there with Princess Nobuko, the eighth daughter of Emperor Meiji. Like many grand buildings in prewar Japan it was subsequently renovated, and reopened to the public on October 1, 1983.

Rapin designed the building to look futuristic, and it still looks futuristic today. The light fixtures are truly remarkable. The Lalique crystal alone, especially the foyer's panels, justifies a visit. The rooms on the second floor look out on gardens that are mediocre by Japanese standards. Most of the visitors do not tour the building but opt to stroll or picnic in the gardens.

Tokyo-to Teien Bijutsukan
5-21-9 Shiroganedai, Minato-ku, Tokyo
Tel: 3443-0201

Hours: 10:00–6:00.
Closed 2nd and 4th Wednesdays of
each month.

Admission: Varies with display,
usually ¥600.

23

ART

美術

40	Setagaya Art Museum	世田谷美術館
41	Sezon Museum of Art	セゾン美術館
42	Shoto Museum	松涛美術館
43	Sogetsu Museum	草月美術館
44	Tokyo Metropolitan Art Museum	東京都立美術館
45	Yamatane Museum of Art	山種美術館

ORIENTAL ART

46	Aizu Memorial Museum of Oriental Arts	早稲田大学 相津博士記念 東洋美術陳列室
47	Century Museum	センチュリー ミュージアム
48	Eisei Bunko Museum	永青文庫
49	Gotoh Museum	五島美術館
50	Hatakeyama Collection	畠山記念館
51	Idemitsu Museum of Art	出光美術館
52	Kurita Museum	栗田美術館
53	Matsuoka Museum of Art	松岡美術館
54	Middle-East Culture Center	中近東 文化センター

PHOTOGRAPHY

SCULPTURE

WESTERN ART

Hasegawa Art Museum

*Shin-Tamagawa Line from Shibuya to Sakura Shinmachi Station,
West Exit. Seven-minute walk.*

Machiko Hasegawa made a fortune creating colorful children's comics. She put some of this money into real estate and art, and avoided the taxman's reach by donating part of her land to establish a museum in Setagaya Ward. Her small collection of European art (including a tiny painting by Marc Chagall) occupies the basement of the museum. Her children's comics adorn the bright gallery walls on the second floor.

Mindful of her likely constituents, Hasegawa installed a video room on the second floor to show children's cartoons. The children pack the place, while some of the parents linger in the basement. Hasegawa is famous in Japan, and the museum is often crowded on weekends. Many curious visitors come to have a gaze at the house next door—Hasegawa's home.

There are many children's museums in Tokyo that equal or surpass the Hasegawa Museum, but it is a pleasant place to spend some time if you are in the Setagaya or Shibuya areas.

Hasegawa Bijutsukan
1-30-6 Sakura Shinmachi, Setagaya-ku, Tokyo
Tel: 3701-8766

Hours: 10:00–5:00.
Closed Monday.
Schedule varies.

Admission: ¥500,
¥400 for high school students,
¥300 for children.

Kumagai Museum

Yurakucho Line to Kanamecho Station. Seven-minute walk.

You won't be able to miss this museum—it has gigantic cement ants embedded in the exterior masonry. It is hard to tell whether this is a museum with an arty coffee shop or a trendy coffee shop with a museum. The proprietor, the daughter of Morikazu Kumagai, has artfully decorated the cafe with ceramics that are for sale. Beautiful Indonesian batiks adorn the tables in the cafe. Tokyo is a city with a thousand pleasant places to drink coffee and gossip, but this is one of the nicest.

The museum consists of two floors and is devoted to Kumagai's works. Many are quite good and have different styles. The collection is rotated frequently and, judging by the storeroom, there is a lot left to show.

Kumagai Morikazu Bijutsukan
2-27-6 Chihaya, Toshima-ku, Tokyo
Tel: 3957-3779

Hours: 10:30–5:30.
Friday, open until 8:00.
Closed Monday.

Admission: ¥500,
¥300 for university students,
¥100 for primary school students.

Kume Museum of Art

Yamanote Line to Meguro Station. Three-minute walk from West Exit. See Map 4.

This small museum is perched on the eighth floor of a sky-scraper. The collection is displayed in a single room, and rotates frequently to make up for the lack of additional space. Classical music gently wafts through the room as you view the works of art and newspaper clippings. The collection is devoted to one artist: Kuchiro Kume, one of the pioneers of Western painting in Japan.

Kume was one of the first Japanese artists to paint in the style of French impressionism. The canvasses are interesting, particularly from a historical perspective. An interesting side-light is a display showing Kume's two-year journey around the world in 1871 and 1872.

A visit to the Kume Museum can be combined with a visit to the Parasitological Museum and the Meguro Museum of Art, all within walking distance of Meguro Station.

Kume Bijutsukan
2-25-5 Kami-Osaki, Shinagawa-ku, Tokyo
Tel: 3491-1510

Hours: 10:00–5:00.
Closed Wednesday.

Admission: ¥500,
¥300 for students.

Mushanokoji Memorial Hall

Keio Line to Senkawa Station. Seven-minute walk.

Don't go to this museum if it is raining because you will not be able to gain entrance to the old house where this writer and painter lived or enjoy the exotic forest. Visitors are not allowed inside when it is muddy.

There are two main buildings to this museum—the writer's home and a modern but small museum which is open in any weather. The museum has a few artifacts, writings, and displays but is outshined by the green forest on the grounds. Take a lovely walk through a bamboo forest, sit by the carp pond, or wander around to see the natural waterfall. It is a great place to read and think great thoughts.

The old home is also interesting. There are many photographs, pieces of old furniture, and artist's materials. The house actually looks lived in and has been faithfully preserved by the curator, the artist's son.

Mushanokoji Saneatsu Kinenkan
1-8-30 Wakabacho, Chofu-shi, Tokyo
Tel: 3326-0648

Hours: 9:00–4:00.   Admission: ¥100,
Closed Monday.   ¥50 for children, free for visitors.

Ryushi Memorial Hall

*Keihin Tohoku Line to Omori Station. West Exit, then bus from
stand 4 to Sakaishita. Two-minute walk.*

Ryushi Kawabata (no relation to author Yasunari Kawabata)
was one of Japan's most distinguished artists. His early works
showed a strong influence from traditional Chinese art.
Toward the end of his life, he developed his own style, painting canvasses utilizing themes of nature. Carp, bamboo, and
examples of the Japanese countryside appear again and again.

Ota Ward has built a huge memorial to Ryushi. The building has a unique design, with a series of rooms connected in an
irregular pattern. Ryushi's early works can be viewed as soon
as you enter the museum, and his final works are displayed in
the last room.

Ryushi's daughter lives across the road in a traditional
Japanese house. Don't make the mistake that we did and
assume that the old house is the museum. The shrill bark of
the dog will dissuade you from any intentions of getting closer.

Ota Kuritsu Ryushi Kinenkan
4-2-1 Chuo, Ota-ku, Tokyo
Tel: 3772-0680

Hours: 9:00–4:30.
Closed Monday.

Admission: ¥200,
¥100 for children.

Yokoyama Memorial Hall

Chiyoda Line to Nezu Station. Ten-minute walk. See Map 2.

The Yokoyama Taikan Memorial is a beautiful Japanese house that was the residence of a venerable Japanese painter. Upon his death, he established a foundation to convert his house into a museum and provide the funding for its maintenance. Like so many Tokyo museums of this type, the building outshines the collection; you will have to work long and hard to find a more beautiful Japanese house and garden.

Unlike many twentieth-century Japanese artists, Yokoyama did not ape Western art styles, but tried to refine traditional Japanese motifs. His paintings have something of a dreamlike quality, with their wide use of soft colors and misty mountains.

Make sure you visit the *shokudō* (dining hall), where the fireplace is located, and have a walk in the peaceful garden, but remember to change your slippers to the outdoor type. The second floor has a good view of the interior courtyard and a spacious atmosphere. Few paintings have made it as far as the second floor.

Yokoyama Taikan Kinenkan
1-4-24 Ikenohata, Taito-ku, Tokyo
Tel: 3821-1017

Hours: 10:00–4:00,
Thursday–Sunday.

Admission: ¥600,
¥500 for students.

Comic Book and Illustration Museum

Chiyoda Line to Nezu Station. Ten-minute walk. See Map 2.

This odd building houses two museums under the same roof. The Yayoi Museum is on the first floor, and the Takehisa Museum is on the second and third floors. You pay one admission price for both museums, which are connected by a small staircase. Both feature Japanese illustrations. The building is located a few meters from the walls of Tokyo University, on the sleepy streets of Nezu. Take your shoes off and wander the small rooms. The first floor has some of the oldest comic books in Japan, while the second and third floors are given over to magazine covers, prints, and Japanese pop art. Most of the old items are displayed under glass in order to preserve the fragile pages.

A tiny Japanese garden is located to the left of the entrance, and a cozy coffee shop occupies the right side. You can see the collection in ten minutes, but spend more time if you can. Where else can you find comic books with Madame Butterfly on the cover?

Yayoi Bijutsukan to Takehisa Yumeji Bijutsukan
2-4-3 Yayoi, Bunkyo-ku, Tokyo
Tel: 3812-0012

Hours: 10:00–5:00.
Closed Monday.

Admission: ¥700,
¥600 for university students,
¥400 for middle and primary school students.

35

Hara Museum of Contemporary Art

Yamanote Line to Shinagawa Station. Thirteen-minute walk.

The Hara Museum provides avant-garde art in a pleasant, art-deco house. It was established in 1979 by the dapper Toshio Hara, an enthusiastic promoter of contemporary art in Japan. The museum is in a beautiful 1938 Bauhaus-style house, encircling a small garden. The fan-shaped building, a product of architect Jin Watanabe, is an important landmark for Japanese architecture buffs.

The exhibit changes regularly; Jasper Johns, Andy Warhol, and Christo, as well as European, Brazilian, and Japanese artists, are well represented. Not all of the exhibits will please visitors, because Hara is not afraid to display truly far-out art.

The Hara Museum publishes a journal in Japanese and English, and sports an unusual gift shop. The shop sells hard-to-find art magazines and books, as well as replicas of some of the exhibits in the permanent collection. The Cafe d'Art, a beautiful place to have a drink or a snack, is housed in an extension designed by Arata Isozaki, one of the hottest architects in the world. Garden seating sprawls out onto the small garden, itself replete with unusual modern art.

Hara Gendai Bijutsukan
4-7-25 Kita-Shinagawa, Shinagawa-ku, Tokyo
Tel: 3445-0651

Hours: 11:00–5:00.
11:00–8:00, Wednesday.
Closed Monday.

Admission: ¥700,
¥500 for students.

JAIB Museum

Toei Shinjuku Line to Shinozaki Station; shuttle bus from the station to the museum.

The JAIB Museum (short for Jack-in-the-box) dares to be different. It is the first museum in Tokyo devoted to trick art—an art form that allows you to touch and feel the paintings while trying to figure out some of the optical illusions they project.

The museum opened on November 3, 1991, and attracts a young crowd. Founded by Yoshiaki Ishii, a driving-school magnate, it displays eighty reproductions of masterpieces from the Louvre Museum. The reproductions were made by Kazumine Kenju, who had to mix his own paint and wrestle with 2,400 different color tones before getting down to work.

The exterior of the museum reproduces one of the Louvre's walls and the entrance is a replica of the Louvre's *Gates of Hell.* The interior is too gloomy for our tastes, but the darkness provides atmosphere for the second-floor cafe, where young couples linger.

Jaibu Bijutsukan
6-136 Shinozaki-machi, Edogawa-ku, Tokyo
Tel: 3678-9966

Hours: 10:00–7:00, Tuesday–Thursday. 10:00–9:00, Fridays, Saturdays, & Sundays.

Admission: ¥800, ¥600 for university students, ¥500 for elementary and junior high school students.

37

National Museum of Modern Art

Tozai Line to Takebashi Station. Two-minute walk. See Map 1.

The National Museum of Modern Art generally attracts some of the best foreign art exhibits to reach the shores of Japan. The René Magritte exhibit in 1988 broke all attendance records and made visitors feel like they were in a subway train rather than an art museum. Less fashionable exhibitions draw small crowds, allowing time to relax and enjoy the classy facilities. The museum's curators are in constant contact with their counterparts around the world, so you can never tell when the next sensation will strike.

The permanent collection is unremarkable by world standards, but still worth a visit. The canvasses by Japanese cubist, impressionist, and op-art artists are particularly interesting. The cheap coffee canteen on the top floor provides a commanding view of the palace moat and Otemachi. Turn in your ticket stub at the ticket counter to receive a free ticket to the National Museum of Modern Art Crafts Gallery down the road.

Tokyo Kokuritsu Kindai Bijutsukan
3 Kitanomaru Koen, Chiyoda-ku, Tokyo
Tel: 3214-2561

Hours: 10:00–5:00.
Closed Monday.

Admission: ¥515, ¥310 for middle school and high school students, ¥205 for children.

Person's Weekend Museum

Bus #81 from Shibuya Station to Sendagaya-Nichome. Three-minute walk.

The Person's Weekend Museum opened in 1991 and specializes in modern art, with an emphasis on American art. The exhibition changes four times a year and is spread over three floors of a new, concrete edifice. The museum has colorful paintings, somewhat offsetting the rather dreary architecture.

The permanent collection includes an impressive roster of canvasses by Frank Stella, David Hockney, and Jasper Johns. Roy Lichtenstein originals also dot the walls. It is a bit surprising to see the original work after viewing so much ersatz Lichtenstein in Japanese advertising.

The museum is small enough to look at every display within a ten-minute visit, but there is a small table and chairs on every floor for an ideal place to take a break, write postcards, or sketch.

The museum is a bit hard to find but is close enough to Harajuku to provide a calm respite from the popular pastime of watching Tokyo's young and restless.

Pasonzu Uikuendo Myujiamu
2-27-16 Jingumae, Shibuya-ku, Tokyo
Tel: 5411-1474

Hours: 2:00–8:00 on Friday, Saturday, and Sunday only.

Admission: ¥700, ¥500 for students.

Setagaya Art Museum

Shin-Tamagawa Line to Yoga Station. Take the local bus from the station.

Think that Tokyo cannot have another glorious, multi-million-dollar museum on splendid grounds? Go to the Setagaya Art Museum. It takes more than one hour to get there from central Tokyo, but it is worth the trip.

This museum is devoted to modern art, and the permanent collection of Japanese modern art is eclectic enough to please most tastes. If you are going to make the trip, and are going to be in Tokyo for any length of time, it is worth calling ahead to try to catch an unusual traveling exhibit.

You can't go wrong visiting here just to see the building and its surroundings. The museum is located on the edge of a huge park, and has a rural atmosphere. The main building sprawls around a futuristic, one-story design, including workshops, a "French" restaurant, a central plaza, lecture halls, a library, and galleries for the permanent and visiting exhibitions. You can rest your feet with a reasonably-priced beverage in the coffee shop on the ground floor. Suffice to say that the Setagaya Art Museum is yet another Tokyo-based, spectacular home for the fine arts, waiting for a collection worthy of its surroundings.

Setagaya Bijutsukan
1-2 Kinuta Koen, Setagaya-ku, Tokyo
Tel: 3415-6011

Hours: 10:00–6:00.
10:00–8:00, Saturday.
Closed 2nd and 4th Mondays.

Admission: Varies with exhibition: ¥200–¥850 for adults, ¥150–¥700 for university students, ¥100–¥500 for children and other students.

40

Sezon Museum of Art

Yamanote Line to Ikebukuro Station. Ten-minute walk.

This museum styles itself as the most important cultural effort of the gigantic Saison Group, the sports, retail, and transportation conglomerate ruled by Yoshiaki Tsutsumi, one of the richest men in the world. The museum is located next to the gigantic flagship of the empire, the Seibu Department Store in Ikebukuro.

The Sezon Museum offers excellent traveling exhibits, and a permanent collection devoted to contemporary and modern art. The museum was renovated and renamed in 1989, and occupies two floors. The obligatory gift shop and cafe are well done and worth a visit.

Unless you are a modern-art buff or a devotee of Tsutsumi's empire, it is better to wait until there is a high-quality visiting exhibition. Seibu has the financial clout to attract the best exhibitions money can buy. For now, the permanent collection is not up to snuff.

Sezon Bijutsukan
1-28-1 Minami-Ikebukuro, Toshima-ku, Tokyo
Tel: 5992-0155

Hours: 10:00–8:00.
Closed Tuesday.

Admission: ¥1100,
¥800 for students, less for some
exhibitions.

41

Shoto Museum

Yamanote Line or Ginza Line to Shibuya Station. Fifteen-minute walk. See Map 4.

The Shoto Museum displays modern Japanese art and traveling exhibits in one of the most unique museum buildings in the world. The building is like a layer cake with a spectacular atrium in the center. Visitors can traverse the atrium via a small bridge overlooking a fountain. All of the galleries look down on the beautiful interior courtyard.

It is a building that you do not want to leave. Be sure to visit all of the floors, even if you are pressed for time. The ground floor—which houses classrooms and restrooms—offers a great view of this architectural masterpiece.

The building clearly outclasses the permanent collection. Artists interested in the Japanese avant-garde may enjoy the collection, but most of it is unremarkable. It is worth waiting for a good traveling exhibit before making the trek to Shibuya.

The Shoto Museum, like the remodelled Courthould Institute in London, allows visitors to relax and have a drink inside one of its exhibition rooms. Allow a little extra time to lounge on the luxuriant leather chairs.

Shoto Bijutsukan
2-14-14 Shoto, Shibuya-ku, Tokyo
Tel: 3465-9421

Hours: 10:00–5:00.
Closed Monday and 1st Sunday of
each month.   Admission: ¥200,
Schedule varies—call ahead to verify.   ¥160 for children and students.

Sogetsu Museum

Ginza or Hanzomon Line to Aoyama-Itchome Station. Three-minute walk. See Map 1.

If you are a fan of ikebana, the Japanese art of flower arranging, a visit to the Sogetsu Building may be like a visit to Mecca. The Sogetsu school of ikebana rejected the doctrinaire teachings of the Kyoto school, revolutionizing the art with modern design. The Sogetsu Building has a wonderful book shop, a spectacular lobby replete with cutting-edge ikebana, and a great view of Akasaka. Unfortunately, the museum does not match this grandeur. However, the cafe overlooking the lobby has bargain-priced coffee. It is a wonderful place to sit and enjoy the flowers.

The museum is on the sixth floor, and consists of one large room where the Sogetsu collection of contemporary art is shown on a rotating basis. Traveling collections can be disappointing, but the permanent collection includes Braque, Warhol, Picasso, and Japanese artists such as Imai and Arakawa.

The Sogetsu Building is still worth a visit. Its neighbors include the spectacular new Canadian Embassy, and a little garden dedicated to Korekiyo Takahashi, possibly the most brilliant politician and economist in Japanese history.

Sogetsu Bijutsukan
7-2-21 Akasaka, Minato-ku, Tokyo
Tel: 3408-1126

Hours: 10:00–5:00.
Closed Sundays.

Admission: ¥500,
¥400 for students.

Tokyo Metropolitan Art Museum

Yamanote Line or other train to Ueno Station. Four-minute walk.
See Map 2.

This museum occupies an impressive building built in 1975. Five times a year the museum hosts a special exhibition sponsored by a major corporation. The emphasis seems to be on contemporary Japanese art.

We were consistently disappointed with the quality of the exhibitions shown here. Many of the artists who have their work shown are mediocre at best. However, there is one thing about this museum that is not mediocre—the library.

The Metropolitan Museum has one of the best art libraries in Asia, housing more than 30,000 items. The reading room seems to have nearly every expensive coffee-table art book you can find at Tokyo book stores. The reading room is free and open to the general public, and is a great place to come and study art.

Tokyo Toritsu Bijutsukan
8-36 Ueno Koen, Taito-ku, Tokyo
Tel: 3823-6921

Hours: 9:00–5:00.
Closed on the 3rd Monday of each
month.   Admission: Free.

Yamatane Museum of Art

Tozai or Hibiya Line to Kayabacho Station. Exits 10, 11 lead you into the first floor of the Yamatane Building. See Map 1.

The Yamatane Museum was opened in 1965 by the Yamatane Group. The museum is devoted to modern Japanese paintings, including works by Seiho Takeuchi, Kagaku Murakami, and Kokei Kobayashi. Unless you are a buff, you can visit during the exhibition of the regular collection, or one of the traveling exhibitions.

The collection occupies the eighth and ninth floors of the Yamatane office building, and provides a fine example of Japanese interior design. The quiet and restful atmosphere is epitomized by the rock garden at the bottom of the stairs on the eighth floor.

A visit to this museum can be combined with the Saturday morning tour at the nearby Tokyo Stock Market or the Tsukiji Fish Market. The Yamatane Museum is not as interesting as Tsukiji or the stock market, but fans of modern art will appreciate a visit.

Yamatane Bijutsukan
7-12 Kabutocho, Nihonbashi, Chuo-ku, Tokyo
Tel: 3669-7643

Hours: 10:00–5:00.
Closed Monday and when
exhibitions are changed.

Admission: ¥600,
¥400 for students.

Aizu Memorial Museum of Oriental Arts at Waseda University

Tozai Line to Waseda Station. Ten-minute walk. See Map 5.

Combine a visit to this museum with the nearby Tsubouchi Theater Museum as both are interesting and have marvelous collections. Like most university museums in Tokyo, Waseda's art museum has many fine pieces displayed in nondescript campus buildings, without the glitz of commercial museums. The pieces are just as beautiful and you don't have to fight the crowds to get a look. The carved miniatures are fantastic.

Waseda is one of the most prestigious universities in Japan, and its graduates are a particularly proud and clubby lot. When Robery F. Kennedy visited Waseda, he turned a crowd of angry demonstrators into his friends by singing the Waseda fight song in broken Japanese. The incident was sensationalized by the Japanese media, and everyone rejoiced—except the graduates of arch-rival Keio University.

Waseda Daigaku Aizu Hakase Kinen
Toyo Bijutsu Chinretsu-shitsu
1-6-1 Nishi-Waseda, Shinjuku-ku, Tokyo
Tel: 3203-4141

Hours: 10:00–5:00.
Closed Saturday and Sunday. Also
closed at irregular intervals; call to
confirm.   Admission: Free.

Century Museum

Marunouchi, Chuo, or Sobu Line to Ochanomizu Station.
Five-minute walk. See Map 2.

The Century Museum is located in the basement of a new sky-scraper. The interior is a bit gloomy, especially after passing through the space-age lobby. One room houses various visiting collections and some of the permanent collection. The other rooms include a library, research room, and museum store.

The permanent collection is small but excellent. Lacquerware, screens, and small bronzes are the best pieces. Even if a traveling exhibit has taken up most of the floor space, browse through the museum store.

Most traveling exhibits that make their way to the Century Museum involve Asian art. Chinese and Southeast Asian antiquities are regular visitors. The Asian accent is interesting, given the modern surroundings, as the majority of museums in Tokyo that concentrate on Asian art tend to be in traditional buildings.

Senchuri Myujiamu
2-2-9 Hongo, Century Tower, Bunkyo-ku, Tokyo
Tel: 5800-0077

Hours: 9:30–4:30.
Closed Sunday.

Admission: ¥500,
¥300 for students.

Eisei Bunko Museum

Yurakucho Line to Edogawabashi Station, Exit 1A. Eight-minute walk.

The outside of the old building is unusual and even spooky. The stucco is peeling and the flora overgrown. The interior is awful—pale lime-green walls and red carpeting—both in need of replacement. Only a few of the rooms are open to the public, but the potential for a great museum is only a brush scrub away.

What draws the crowds to this place is the superb collection of Japanese and Chinese antiques. There are excellent porcelains and watercolors which would make any major Japanese museum envious. The collection is extensive and must be rotated frequently due to the lack of "proper" display rooms. The built-in bookcases and cabinets of solid wood make the displays more homey. If they would just get rid of the peeling paint, trim a few bushes, and recarpet, this museum would be a knockout.

Eisei Bunko
1-1-1 Mejiro-dai, Bunkyo-ku, Tokyo
Tel: 3491-0850

Hours: 10:00–4:30 Monday–Friday,
and on 2nd and 4th Saturday of each
month.

Admission: ¥400,
¥200 for students.

Gotoh Museum

Tokyu Oimachi Line to Kaminoge Station. Three-minute walk.

If you like beautiful gardens, tea rooms, and scenic views of Tokyo, then the Gotoh Museum is a must. Schedule your visit on a clear day so that you can wander through its huge gardens. Many old stone statues and ponds adorn the walks. Bring comfortable walking shoes since many of the walks are on a steep incline.

The museum is built atop a bluff so it affords visitors a nice view of Tokyo. After your stroll, try your hand at a tea ceremony in one of the many tea houses—this museum seems to do standing room only with tea. However, the staff are less receptive to foreign visitors than at the Nezu Museum, which also sells the tea-ceremony experience.

The museum was founded by the Tokyu Department Store group. Like so many museums of this type, the gardens outshine the collection of silk-screens, bronzes, and woodblock prints indoors. The collection is rotated frequently and judging from its art books, which are sold at the entrance, there are many interesting pieces.

Gotoh Bijutsukan
3-9-25 Kaminoge, Setagaya-ku, Tokyo
Tel: 3703-0661

Hours: 9:30–4:30.
Closed Monday.

Admission: ¥500,
¥350 for students.

49

Hatakeyama Collection

Toei Asakusa Line to Takanawadai Station. Six-minute walk.
See Map 3.

If you want to go to Kyoto but can't spare the time, this may be one of the best substitutes in Tokyo. The Hatakeyama Collection is located on beautifully landscaped grounds in a quiet neighborhood. Be sure to allow time to walk along the winding trails. Peeking out from the medieval landscape are traditional Japanese houses. These houses are actually classy and expensive traditional Japanese restaurants. You may have to take out a second mortgage to eat there, but they are a lovely sight.

The museum itself gives you the feeling you are in an enclave of old Japanese culture. Remove your shoes, admire the lovely foyer, and pad up the stairs to the exhibition room on the second floor. The exhibition changes completely in the spring and in the fall. At any time, there are fifty exquisite examples of old Japanese pottery, lacquerware, scrolls, and other antiques, as well as even more ancient Chinese pieces. The collection is particularly strong in items from the Edo period when Japan was largely closed to Western influence. The exhibition room has a tiny indoor garden and some pretty tatami rooms with large hanging scrolls.

Hatakeyama Kinenkan
2-20-12 Shirogane-dai, Minato-ku, Tokyo
Tel: 3447-5787

Hours: 10:00–4:30.
Closed Monday.

Admission: ¥500,
¥350 for all students.

Idemitsu Museum of Art

Hibiya Line to Hibiya Station. Exit B3 is located next to the elevator bank leading to the museum. See Map 1.

No museum in Tokyo boasts a more beautiful view than the Idemitsu Museum of Art. One of the exhibition rooms looks down on the Imperial Palace and Hibiya Park. Complimentary tea is provided, as well as chairs for rest and relaxation.

The Idemitsu Museum opened in 1966 to house the private collection of Sazo Idemitsu, the petroleum magnate and art collector. His original interest in Japanese calligraphy and ceramics broadened to include Oriental antiquities and Western art.

If you don't get sidetracked by the view, you will have an opportunity to see a fine, eclectic collection of art. The rotating exhibits concentrate on Oriental antiquities and a large collection of paintings by the French artist Georges-Henri Roualt. This odd combination was made possible by the museum's purchase of over four hundred of Roualt's works in 1972. Roualt's canvasses show the influence of Chagall and Matisse. His early works depict prostitutes, clowns, and judges, while his later works concentrate on religious themes. Some of the paintings are reminiscent of stained glass and mosaics.

Idemitsu Bijutsukan
Kokusai Building, 9th Floor, 3-1-1 Marunouchi,
Chiyoda-ku, Tokyo
Tel: 3213-9402

Hours: 10:00–5:00.
Closed Mondays.

Admission: ¥500,
¥300 for students.

51

Kurita Museum

Hibiya Line to Ningyocho Station. Five-minute walk. See Map 1.

This little museum is devoted to Japanese porcelain. The collection is not nearly as good as the collection at the Toguri Museum of Art, but it is a quiet and pleasant place to visit.

Hideo Kurita began collecting porcelain in earnest during the postwar period. He set up operations near an American base, buying back pieces that soldiers had bought at bargain prices. Most of Kurita's extensive collection is housed outside of Tokyo; only a few pieces have found a home in Nihonbashi.

The collection is located on the top floor of what is otherwise a nondescript building. There are chairs that allow you to sit down and browse through the fancy books on the table, comparing pictures in the book to the specimens in the collection.

Kurita Bijutsukan
2-17-9 Nihonbashi Hamacho, Chuo-ku, Tokyo
Tel: 3666-6246

Admission: ¥500,
¥300 for students
Hours: 10:00–5:00 (except university students).

Matsuoka Museum of Art

Mita Line to Onarimon Station, Exit A4. Two-minute walk.
See Map 3.

This museum was started by one of the richest real estate magnates in Japan, and occupies two floors in a skyscraper in central Tokyo. The museum is organized in an unusual loft style, which allows for distant views of the exhibits on the first floor.

The first floor has many priceless pieces of ancient art, including an Egyptian sarcophagus, Chinese bronzes, and stone statues from India and Cambodia. There are literally no weak exhibits on the first floor. This is unusual in museums of this type, which often have spectacular surroundings but collections that do not live up to the physical plant. This criticism cannot be made about the Matsuoka.

The second floor is a bit of a letdown, but worth a quick look. Modern Japanese paintings are interspersed with Edo-era woodblock prints. Few of the items are outstanding. People most interested in ancient art, particularly from Egypt and India, will get the most out of a visit.

A visit to the Matsuoka Museum can be combined with a visit to Tokyo Tower, the American Club, or the NHK Broadcast Museum. It is close enough to most of the locations in central Tokyo to make a spur of the moment or lunch-time visit feasible.

Matsuoka Bijutsukan
5-22-10 Shinbashi, Minato-ku, Tokyo
Tel: 3437-2787

Hours: 10:00–5:00.
Closed Monday.

Admission: ¥550,
¥200 for students.

Middle-East Culture Center

Chuo Line to Musashi Sakai Station, bus #1 from platform 4 to Nishino stop. Ten-minute walk.

This museum is devoted to art and antiquities of the Middle East, and is housed in one of the most beautiful museum buildings in all of Japan. Exhibition Hall No. 1 includes pottery and other antiquities from ancient Egypt, Mesopotamia, and surrounding regions, and includes artifacts over 5,000 years old. Exhibits in Hall No. 2 trace the evolution of Islamic pottery.

There is a sitting room with comfortable couches in front of floor-to-ceiling windows. It is a wonderful spot to sip the complimentary tea, and leaf through the remarkable books in the cases nearby while gazing out onto beautiful Japanese gardens. The second floor contains one of the best Middle-Eastern libraries in Asia, but you must be a member to use the facilities. Unfortunately, it seems to be one of the most seldom visited museums in the Tokyo area. Go while the elbow room lasts, so you can be alone with the mystery of ancient cultures.

A visit to this museum should be coupled with a visit to the beautiful campus of International Christian University and the Yuasa Memorial Museum, less than a four-minute walk from the front door.

Chukinto Bunka Senta
3-10-31 Ohsawa, Mitaka-shi, Tokyo
Tel: 0422-32-7111

Hours: 10:00–5:00.
Closed Monday.

Admission: ¥300,
¥200 for students.

Mitsui Museum

Seibu Shinjuku Line to Araiyakushimae Station. Four-minute walk.

Mitsui is one of the largest trading companies in the world, and a primary engine of Japan's economic miracle. Some of Mitsui's profits were plowed into an art collection, now housed in a quiet park in affluent Nakano Ward.

The museum is particularly strong in Japanese paintings from the Muromachi era (1333–1568). The sixteenth-century paintings hail from a time when most Japanese art was an imitation of Chinese art, although these imitations are excellent.

Unfortunately, the collection does not give the visitor the opportunity to compare the Muromachi paintings with paintings from the period of seclusion during the Edo period (1600–1868). Many collections around the world, including one at the University of Michigan, provide such an opportunity. During the period of seclusion, Japanese art evolved away from Chinese imitation to find its own style.

Don't miss the fine video shown in the basement. It is one of the best videos on Japanese art at any museum in Tokyo.

Mitsui Bunko Bijutsukan
5-16-1 Kami-Takada, Nakano-ku, Tokyo
Tel: 3387-2211

Hours: 10:00–4:00.
Closed Monday. Call to verify.

Admission: ¥500,
¥300 for university students,
¥200 for primary and middle school
students.

55

Nezu Museum

Chiyoda or Ginza Line to Omotesando Station, Exit A5. Ten-minute walk. See Map 4.

The Nezu Museum, like many museums in Tokyo, was founded by a rich man who left the museum as part of his legacy to the world. In terms of aesthetics, this attempt is particularly successful. The complex occupies some of the most expensive real estate in the world, near Harajuku Station, in one of Tokyo's tonier districts.

The founder used his money to indulge his eclectic tastes in art. He started out a Sinophile, and ended up collecting one of the world's best exhibits of objects relating to tea and the Japanese tea ceremony. The Nezu Museum also picked up several marvelous private collections.

You may not care for the traveling exhibits, or for the splendid permanent collection of Chinese bronzes and screens, but you won't be able to pass up walking through the 21,627 square meters that surround the main buildings. The gardens and hiking opportunities are spectacular.

The grounds are dotted with seven traditional tea houses. Exhibitions of the tea ceremony can be seen in the largest tea house on national holidays and other days. Call for the latest schedule.

Nezu Bijutsukan
6-5-1 Minami-Aoyama, Minato-ku, Tokyo
Tel: 3400-2536

Hours: 9:30–4:30.
Closed Monday.

Admission: ¥1000,
¥700 for students.

Ota Memorial Museum of Art

Yamanote Line to Harajuku or Ginza Line to Omotesando.
Ten-minute walk. See Map 4.

The Ota Museum is one of the few museums in Tokyo devoted to one of the great Japanese artistic traditions—the woodblock print. The Japanese turned away from this art form after the Meiji Restoration, and many of the best pieces were snapped up by foreigners. The Art Institute of Chicago may have a collection superior to any museum in Japan.

Lovers of *hanga* (woodblock prints) will like the Ota Museum, others will be disappointed. The display space is small and divided over two floors. The entrance and some of the interior furnishings are done in traditional Japanese style. The low lighting may contribute to the medieval atmosphere the museum hopes to achieve, but for some, it may hinder viewing.

The Ota Museum has a permanent collection and provides a home to traveling exhibitions. If possible, visit the Do! Family Art Museum just up the street. The collection of woodblock prints by the French artist Paul Joculet will make an interesting comparison to the Ota collection.

Ota Kinen Bijutsukan
1-10-10 Jingumae, Shibuya-ku, Tokyo
Tel: 3403-0880

Hours: 10:30–5:30.
Closed Monday and for a few days at
the end of each month.

Admission ¥800,
¥700 for students.

57

Riccar Museum

Subway to Ginza Station, Exit C2. Five-minute walk. See Map 1.

This would be a great museum if they would turn the lights on. The tiny Riccar Museum is one of the few Tokyo museums devoted to woodblock prints. The exhibit changes monthly, and features prints of one artist. However, the exhibition room is so gloomy you cannot get a good look at the prints.

The Riccar Museum is conveniently located in the swish Ginza area, making it suitable for a quick visit during a short trip to Tokyo. Hardcore fans of *ukiyo-e*, or woodblock prints representing "the floating world" of Japan, will want to plan repeat visits. The best time to visit is December, when prints of the incomparable Kitagawa Utamaro are displayed.

The Ota Memorial Museum of Art in Harajuku has a more attractive way of presenting woodblock prints, but the Riccar Museum has a superb collection. So many museums in Tokyo have spectacular surroundings, but no collection to speak of. Sadly, the Riccar Museum is the opposite.

Rikka Bijutsukan
6-2-3 Ginza, Chuo-ku, Tokyo
Tel: 3571-3254

Hours: 11:00–6:00.
Closed Monday, and occasional
one-week periods when exhibitions
change.

Admission: ¥300,
¥200 for students.

Shinjuku Museum

Marunouchi Line to Shinjuku Gyoenmae. Four-minute walk.

The Shinjuku Museum is located in the basement of a nondescript building on a nondescript street. The museum is open by request only; call from the phone booth across the street, and the curator will get out her keys.

The museum houses the private collection of dolls and Chinese antiques amassed by one of Tokyo's many real-estate tycoons who obviously put a lot of money into the tiny museum. Marble and glass have transformed a dull little Shinjuku basement into a pretty place.

Although nearly every visitor to Tokyo passes through Shinjuku, the area around Shinjuku Station, the mother of all train stations, has surprizingly few museums. This humble little museum is a step in the right direction.

As we signed the register the curator clucked "Tokyo must be getting international if the foreigners are finding out about places like this."

Shinjuku Bijutsukan
1-34-3 Shinjuku, Shinjuku-ku, Tokyo
Tel: 3355-0550

Hours: 10:00–4:00,
Tuesday–Friday.

Admission: ¥300.

59

Toguri Museum of Art

Yamanote Line or subway to Shibuya Station. Ten-minute walk.
See Map 4.

If you like antique porcelain, you will love this museum. The collection alternates displays of Chinese and Japanese porcelain, and only one is shown at any given time. Both are spectacular and justify a visit.

The Toguri Museum is spread over two floors, with a video display room, garden, and offices on the first floor. The marble staircase, complete with glass display cases set into the wall, make climbing stairs enjoyable. There are many lovely details throughout the museum; even the bathroom door handles are decorative porcelain. The museum is a good place to relax and catch your breath after the insanity of Shibuya Station. Even the walk to the museum through the fashionable neighborhood is a delight.

At any given time, approximately one hundred pieces of fine porcelain are on display. They run the gamut from early, crude works to items so exquisite that a magnifying glass is placed in front of a piece to allow visitors to admire the detail. Most of the Japanese pieces hail from Imari, in Kyushu. Legend has it that French artisans copied techniques from Kerala, India and Imari in fashioning the remarkable Limoges porcelain.

Toguri Bijutsukan
1-11-3 Shoto, Shibuya-ku, Tokyo
Tel: 3465-0070

Hours: 10:00–5:00.

Admission: ¥1030, ¥730 for all students.

Tokyo National Museum

Yamanote Line or other train to Ueno Station. Four-minute walk.
See Map 2.

This is the flagship of the fleet, probably the largest and most comprehensive museum in all of Japan. The 88,000 items in the collection are housed in several different buildings. It would take several days to see everything that this museum has to offer.

The collection is particularly strong in the fields of Japanese painting, sculpture, calligraphy, textiles, and archaeology. The collection includes eighty-three items registered as *kokuhō* (national treasures), as well as hundreds of other priceless pieces.

The oldest building provides the best atmosphere in the complex, but not necessarily the best pieces. We were disappointed in the collection of woodblock prints. However, no other museum in Tokyo has a better collection of lacqerware and antiques.

The Tokyo National Museum has a great gift shop, and attracts excellent traveling exhibitions from museums around the world. Don't miss this museum.

Tokyo Kokuritsu Hakubutsukan
13-9 Ueno Koen, Taito-ku, Tokyo
Tel: 3822-1111

Admission: ¥400,
¥130 for university and high school
students, ¥70 for primary and
Hours: 9:00–4:30.   middle school students.

Tokyo University Museum of Art

Inokashira Line from Shibuya to Komaba Todaimae Station.
Two-minute walk. See Map 4.

The old building is nothing much, but the lively freshman and sophomore Todai students—Japan's future government and business elite—are interesting to observe. The museum seems to be an afterthought, but the old Japanese and Chinese artifacts are mildly interesting. You would think some hot-shot Todai alumni would donate some money or artwork befitting the reputation of the university.

The quadrangle is reminiscent of the Ivy League colleges in the United States and worth a stroll. You can then see the Todai students before they change campuses and pass through the red gate of the Hongo campus. By that time they are juniors, and their period of prolonged relaxation is already drawing to a close. The Japan Folk Crafts Museum is nearby, so why not visit both?

Tokyo Daigaku Hakubutsukan
3-8-1 Komaba, Meguro-ku, Tokyo
Tel: 3467-1171

Hours: 10:00–4:00, Wednesday–
Friday.   Admission: Free.

Tomioka Museum

Keihin Tohoku Line to Omori Station, West Exit. Four-minute walk.

A small collection of Chinese, Korean, and Japanese pottery, sculptures, and paintings on silk are displayed in this small but pretty house.

The garden is nothing special and unless the second floor is open, the visitor does not see much during one visit.

There are three main exhibition areas and a tatami room with display cases. The rooms are small but the largest room has higher than usual ceilings. The special exhibit of tea ceremony bowls brings the kimono-clad *sensei* (teachers) out of their tea rooms. People-watching may compensate for what is otherwise a rather mediocre collection.

Tomioka Bijutsukan
2-13-3 Sanno, Ota-ku, Tokyo
Tel: 3771-5100

Hours: 10:00–4:00.

Admission: ¥350,
¥250 students (except university).

Tokyo Metropolitan Museum of Photography

Yamanote Line to Ebisu Station, East Exit. Five-minute walk.
See Map 4.

This museum is the first museum in Japan to specialize in photographic exhibitions. The museum was opened in June 1990, and will relocate to larger quarters in 1993. For the time being the museum occupies a modern, steel and glass structure on a sleepy street near Ebisu Station.

The museum exhibits numerous collections of contemporary photography. Much of what is shown is of recent vintage. Some could be classified as avant-garde. Photography buffs will love the museum; others may think it is a bore. Both groups will enjoy the relative tranquility of Ebisu.

The new museum will include a wing called the Experimental Visual Space. It promises to be an interesting experience. This space will be devoted to the newest visual expressions in computer art and graphics. This wing alone may justify a visit.

Tokyo-to Shashin Bijutsukan
4-19-24 Ebisu, Shibuya-ku, Tokyo
Tel: 3280-0031

Hours: 10:00–6:00.
Closed 2nd and 4th Wednesdays of
the month.

Admission: ¥500,
¥250 for students
(except university).

Asakura Choso Memorial Museum

Yamanote or Keisei Line to Nippori Station, West Exit.
See Map 2.

This museum is the house of Fumio Asakura, one of Japan's most celebrated sculptors. Asakura died in 1964, and his house was renovated and opened as a museum on December 1, 1986. The house is composed of spectacular rooms spread over three floors: the Tea Ceremony Room (first floor), the Poised Mind Room (second floor), and the Morning Sun Room (third floor).

The house is built around a serene Japanese garden that can be viewed from virtually every room. Asakura's statues are nothing special, but the rooms, decorations, and garden are truly spectacular. Few museums in Tokyo provide the splendid ambience of the Asakura Museum. Unfortunately, the curators are particularly paranoid about visiting foreigners. You can anticipate being followed throughout the museum.

The Asakura Museum is located in one of the oldest neighborhoods in Tokyo. There are more than ten temples within walking distance of the museum, and even the alleys and small shops are redolent of old Edo.

Asakura Choso-kan
7-18-10 Yanaka, Taito-ku, Tokyo
Tel: 3821-4549

Hours: 9:30–4:30.
Closed Monday and Friday.

Admission: ¥300,
¥150 for primary and high school students.

65

Contemporary Sculpture Museum

Toyoko Line from Shibuya to Yutenji, bus bound for Naka-Meguro to Shizen-En-Shita stop. Three-minute walk. Also, Hibiya or Toyoko Line to Naka-Meguro, twenty-minute walk. See Map 4.

Just when we were getting sick of visiting every museum in Tokyo, we were lucky enough to visit this museum. It has everything—a great location, impressive quarters and a decent collection.

Stockholm's Milles Garden is the closest thing to the Contemporary Sculpture Museum. Both museums have a quiet suburban location and many sturdy sculptures out of doors; neither museum is going to be overrun with tourists. The Milles Garden has a better collection, but it is 10,000 kilometers away. If you are in Tokyo and you are interested in modern sculpture, the Contemporary Sculpture Museum is a must.

The main building has a nice coffee shop and two floors of sculptures, ranging from the modern to the futuristic. There is plenty to see even if it is raining and you can't lounge in the adjoining garden.

Gendai Chokoku Bijutsukan
4-12-18 Naka-Meguro, Meguro-ku, Tokyo
Tel: 3792-5858

Hours: 10:00–5:00.
Closed Monday.   Admission: Free.

Okura Museum

Ginza Line to Toranomon. Ten-minute walk to main entrance of Hotel Okura. See Map 1.

The museum is housed in a traditional Japanese-style building located in front of the main entrance of the Hotel Okura—the epitome of Westernization in Japan. The museum is surrounded by a tiny, beautiful Japanese garden. The surrounding skyscrapers provide a stunning backdrop to the stone Buddha sitting in the garden.

The museum houses the small but splendid collection of Oriental statues collected by the Okura Foundation, founded in 1917 to prevent Japanese art treasures from leaving the country. Much of the original collection was destroyed in the catastrophic Great Kanto Earthquake of 1923. The remainder survive in a building designed to withstand the next gigantic quake. So far, it has not been put to the test.

Some visitors think that the old, musty building is unattractive and a bit run down. However, the old building contributes to the atmosphere for viewing the spectacular Buddhist statues and artwork. Particularly remarkable are the stone statute from the fifth century and the stone lion from China's sixth dynasty. A beautiful seated Shakyamuni, his hand damaged in the quake, stares into space at the far end of the first floor.

Okura Shukokan
2-10-3 Toranomon, Minato-ku, Tokyo
Tel: 3583-0781

Hours: 10:00–4:00.

Admission: ¥400,
¥300 for students,
¥150 for children.

Bridgestone Museum

Ginza Line to Kyobashi or Nihonbashi Station. The museum is on the second floor of the Bridgestone Building, midway between the above two stations. Five-minute walk. See Map 1.

When we first came to Japan, few art dealers knew or cared about the Japanese market. However, in the late 1980s, the Japanese were the financial force behind the spectacular increase in the price of fine art, especially French impressionists. Every big Japanese corporation worth its salt purchased an impressionist painting or two. However, it was not always this way. Twenty years ago, there was only one place in Asia that had a creditable impressionist collection—the Bridgestone Museum. Today, the Bridgestone Museum is a must-see for anyone with a love of impressionist art.

The collection spans two floors, and has at least one example of every major French impressionist artist. The Bridgestone also has the best collection of Japanese impressionists in the world. Anyone who has marvelled at the Australian impressionists at the National Gallery in Melbourne, Victoria, or the American impressionists at the Art Institute in Chicago, has to visit the Bridgestone.

Burijisuton Bijutsukan
1-10 Kyobashi, Chuo-ku, Tokyo
Tel: 3563-0241

Hours: 10:00–5:30.
Closed Monday.

Admission: ¥500,
students ¥400.

Do! Family Art Museum

Chiyoda Line to Meiji Jingumae Station, Exit 2. Five-minute walk.
See Map 4.

Tired of shopping on ritzy Omotesando-dori? This new museum is located just behind the shopping mecca. The Do! Family Art Museum was founded by a major clothing company. Their budget-priced clothes bear the motto "Proudly made in Japan." If you don't like museums you can visit their anchor store just behind the museum.

The museum boasts a collection of over 150 woodblock prints by the French artist Paul Jacoulet, who lived in Japan in the 1930s. Of more notoriety are the art works (not proudly made in Japan) of Joan Miro, Pablo Picasso, Marc Chagall, Henri Matisse, and Toulouse Lautrec. The Georges Roualt art is no match for the collection at the Idemitsu Museum. Everything is translated into French and English. The museum's new architecture does not compete with the art—the stark white walls, parquet wood, stone floors, and open spaces are a little dull. The canned classical muzak does nothing to liven up the place.

The museum is located on an old street newly named "Museum Street." The Ota Museum is just around the corner and the Shaving Culture Museum is only a few blocks away.

Do Famiri Bijutsukan
1-12-4 Jingumae, Shibuya-ku, Tokyo
Tel: 3470-4540

Hours: 11:00–7:30.
Closed Monday.

Admission: ¥800,
¥600 for college and high school
students, ¥300 for middle school
and primary school students.

Kawamura Memorial Museum of Art

Keisei or Narita Line to Sakura Station. Free shuttle bus from station to the museum.

Chiba Prefecture, the "New Jersey of Japan," does not give up its secrets easily. Most foreigners ram through the place on the way to or from Narita Airport. The next time you do this, give Chiba a chance; it is home to the Kawamura Memorial Museum.

The museum is located on a billion-dollar plot of real estate with plenty of trees. The tiny collection is oriented toward modern artists such as Kandinsky, Chagall, and Pollock. The museum claims to have one of the world's largest collections of Frank Stella sculptures, but this is a dubious honor. Many of the sculptures look like decorated garbage cans.

Better bets include Rembrandt's *Portrait of a Man in a Broad-Brimmed Hat,* and Renoir's *Baigneuse.* A splendid Monet or Picasso will make you glad you made the trip. By all means combine this museum with the nearby National Museum of Japanese History.

Kawamura Kinenkan
631 Sakado, Sakura-shi, Chiba 285
Tel: 0434-98-2131

Hours: 10:30–4:30,
Wednesday–Sunday.

Admission: ¥800,
¥600 for high school and university students, ¥400 for primary and middle school students.

National Museum of Western Art

Yamanote Line or other train to Ueno Station. Three-minute walk. See Map 2.

This is one of the most popular museums in Tokyo, and with good reason. The National Museum of Western Art, located across from the Bunka Kaikan concert hall in Ueno Park, has one of the best collections of Western art in all of Asia. The collection is not as broad as the best museums in Europe or North America, but most of the major forces in Western art are represented.

The museum also attracts some of the best traveling exhibitions the world has to offer. The El Greco exhibit in 1986 is one example of a special exhibition that captured the public's fancy and had the turnstiles ringing.

Even short time visitors to Tokyo usually make it to Ueno Park. Don't miss this museum.

Kokuritsu Seiyo Bijutsukan
7-7 Ueno Koen, Taito-ku, Tokyo
Tel: 3828-5131

Hours: 9:30–5:00.
Closed Monday.

Admission: ¥790,
¥450 for university and high school
students, ¥250 for primary and
middle school students.

71

Yasuda Museum of Art

Any train line to Shinjuku Station, West Exit. Five-minute walk.
See Map 5.

This museum's principal claim to fame is its acquisition of Van Gogh's *Sunflowers,* at a record-breaking purchase of 5.3 billion yen, that put the huge Yasuda Company on the art-world map. The museum is perched on the forty-second floor of the head office, with one of the best views of Tokyo. On a clear day, the spectacular view justifies the admission price. Keep this admonition in mind. Aside from a few impressionists, there is nothing special in the collection. However, Mr. Gotoh, the company president, has stated that he would like to fill about one third of the museum with Western impressionists. Look out Sothebys.

The lion's share of the collection is various works by Seiji Togo, hardly one of Japan's best artists. The permanent collection also includes twenty-eight paintings by Grandma Moses, two Renoirs, a Cezanne, and a Gauguin. Unfortunately, almost all paintings are displayed in rather gloomy interior rooms. This is one time that the Japanese flair for presentation seems to have fizzled.

The Cezanne, the Gauguin, and *Sunflowers* are displayed behind bulletproof glass in a dark room. The controversy surrounding the acquisition of *Sunflowers* explains the bulletproof glass.

Yasuda Bijutsukan
Yasuda Fire and Marine Headquarters Building, 42nd floor,
1-26-1 Nishi-Shinjuku, Shinjuku-ku, Tokyo
Tel: 3349-3081

Hours: 9:30–5:00.
Closed Monday.

Admission: ¥500,
¥300 for high school and college
students, ¥200 for children.

Yokohama Museum of Art

JR to Sakuragicho Station. Four-minute walk.

The Yokohama Museum of Art has a truly spectacular building, and a collection that is trying to catch up. The permanent collection includes works by Cezanne, Picasso, Mapplethorpe, and Francis Bacon. However, noteworthy pieces of art are scarce.

This impressive museum opened in November 1989 on the waterfront of Yokohama. Huge fountains occupy part of the plaza in front of the museum. The entrance leads to a "Grand Gallery" worthy of its name. An immense glass ceiling provides natural light for marble staircases and grecian columns. The exhibition rooms look down into the immense foyer.

We were surprised to see a traveling collection of Gauguin works poorly displayed in dim rooms. The rest of the museum seems to have spared no expense, but the best art in the place was hidden in a room with a distinctly makeshift feel to it. This poor planning can easily be corrected because the other exhibition rooms are excellent.

Yokohama Bijutsukan
3-4-1 Minato Mirai, Nishi-ku, Yokohama
Tel: 045-221-0300

Admission: ¥500,
¥300 for high school and university
students, ¥100 for primary and
Hours: 10:00–6:00.   middle school students.

COSTUME
&
FASHION

衣装

Ace World-Bag Museum

Toei Asakusa Line to Asakusa Station, Exit A1. Twenty-second walk.
See Map 2.

This museum is so rarely visited that you are told how to turn on the lights when you go upstairs on the elevator. Unlike some museums that are cutting corners, this museum has a wonderful collection.

There are hundreds of bags grouped by country, and we were surprised to see how many countries make first-class luggage. France produced the best pieces in the museum, but Germany, China, Mexico, and the US are not that far behind. Mexico and China produce some of the best leather pieces with intricate details, while the Americans excel at functional, futuristic bags.

The old bags are interesting, especially the big steamer trunks used on ocean liners in days of yore. However, most of the collection is of recent vintage. The museum sparkles with newness, and has the fresh smell of leather everywhere.

Esu Sekai no Kabankan
1-8-10 Komagata, Taito-ku, Tokyo
Tel: 3847-5515

Hours: 10:00–4:30, Monday–
Friday. Call to confirm.   Admission: Free.

Button Museum

Toei Asakusa Line to Higashi-Nihonbashi Station. Five-minute walk.
See Map 1.

The Button Museum is a place with a humble name but a grand realization. Perched on the fourth floor of a building overlooking the Sumida River, the museum resembles an eighteenth-century drawing room, with moldings and antique lamps dotting the display cases. The foyer sports a grand room with plush leather furniture. A fifteen-minute video about the museum airs regularly. Watch it here, because the tiny gift shop charges ¥5,500 for the tape.

The compact subject matter provides for a great collection in a small place. The Chanel buttons are remarkable. Gold and silver buttons abound. The value of the collection may account for the paranoid reaction of the staff. Japanese visitors who viewed the videotape with us must have ratted to the management that *gaijin* (foreigners) were about; perspiring staff arrived shortly thereafter. The awkward moments that ensued cut short an otherwise delightful afternoon.

Botan no Hakubutsukan
Iris Building 4th floor, 1-11-8 Hamacho, Nihonbashi, Tokyo
Tel: 3864-6537

Hours: 10:00–5:00, Monday–
Friday. Appointment necessary.   Admission: ¥300.

Iwasaki Fashion Institute Museum

Bus #11 from Sakuragicho Station. Bus stop is in front of museum.

This is one of the most beautiful museum buildings in Yokohama and the collection is just as grand. Located in the fashionable Yamate area, where competition between beautiful museums is fierce, this one fits the neighborhood well. The collection comprises art-deco glassware and period costumes and is displayed in a marbled two-story showroom. The Lalique glass is fantastic.

The period dresses are exquisite copies of original designs and are in full and doll sizes. You can even try on an old-fashioned dress and have your picture taken by the professional photographer on the premises. After your hectic fitting, relax and have a cup of tea in the charming parlor, complete with etched-glass windows and Victorian-style over-stuffed chairs. Pass the crumpets please.

Iwasaki Hakubutsukan
254 Yamatecho, Naka-ku, Yokohama
Tel: 045-623-2111

Hours: 9:40–6:00.
Closed Monday.

Admission: ¥300,
¥100 for children.

Princess Gallery Handbag Museum

Toei Asakusa Line to Asakusabashi Station, Exit A5. Two-minute walk. See Map 1.

The museum is dark, and it may be a bit hard to get the nervous staff to give you the badge necessary for entry to the sanctum sanctorum, but it is worth it. The collection is simply outstanding. Purses and bags from forty countries are balanced by the best new work Japan has to offer.

The most interesting pieces are from distant countries such as Zaire and Uzbekistan. The purses from far-flung Indonesian isles are equally intriguing.

The dark museum is not dank. The air crackles with a fresh, clean smell of leather. The marble walls and fixtures must have cost a fortune. The sponsoring corporation obviously does have a fortune. Otherwise, it would not be burying millions of yen in a tax shelter that few people know about and hardly anyone visits.

Fukuromono Sankokan
2-4-1 Asakusabashi, Taito-ku, Tokyo
Tel: 3862-2111

Hours: 10:00–4:00,
Monday–Friday.   Admission: Free.

Sugino Gakuen Costume Museum

JR to Meguro Station. Five-minute walk.

This museum is located in an impressive building on a quiet street in Meguro, near St. Anselm's Benedictine church. The collection sprawls over four floors, and is devoted to the history of gowns and dresses.

There is a vaguely dilapidated atmosphere to the museum. The floors are linoleum, the lighting florescent, and the hallways are dreary and a bit dank. The couches and chairs on the second floor are wrapped in slipcovers. Many of the antique gowns are not in the best shape; a cat seems to have gotten at some of them. The mannequins are enclosed in dusty glass cases.

A tiny "theater" plays a television documentary about the evolution of female attire. Smaller collections of men's clothing, and traditional dresses from Southeast Asian countries, are modeled on the third and fourth floor. You can see the whole collection in twenty minutes.

Sugino Gakuen Isho Hakubutsukan
4-6-19 Kami-Osaki, Shinagawa-ku, Tokyo
Tel: 3491-8151

Hours: 10:00–4:00.
Closed Sundays and from mid-
August to mid-September.

Admission: ¥200,
¥100 for primary and secondary
school students.

Tabi Museum

Sobu Line to Ryogoku Station. Eight-minute walk. See Map 6.

Tabi are the split-toed white socks worn with traditional Japanese footwear such as *geta*. Demand for *tabi* waned as Western fashions gained ascendance, but Sumida Ward is a traditional place, and old traditions live on. The Tabi Museum is a tiny memorial in the front of a store that specializes in making *tabi*.

The store has some of the most illustrious customers in Japan. The Ryogoku Kokugikan (sumo stadium) is nearby, and the most famous sumo wrestlers in Japan shop here. The great Chiyonofuji's *tabi* are displayed here, along with Onokuni's and Asahifuji's. The largest *tabi* displayed is from Konishiki, the American sumo wrestler who gave up a music scholarship to Syracuse University to follow the footlights in Ryogoku.

Tabi have a nascent following among Westerners, as they provide comfortable footwear for lounging around the house. They make a nice, cheap souvenir to bring home from Japan.

Tabi Shiryokan
1-9-3, Midori, Sumida-ku, Tokyo
Tel: 3631-0092

Hours: 9:00–6:00.   Admission: Free.

Tokyo Tower Wax Museum

Hibiya Line to Kamiyacho Station. Ten-minute walk. See Map 3.

Like many things made in Japan, this museum is an exact copy of something in the West. It is glitzy and kitsch, but well done and worth a visit.

The first exhibit shows *Chūshingura,* the Kabuki play commemorating the story of the forty-seven ronin. This was the only play banned by the Allied Occupation because it was a symbol of the desire for revenge on the part of some elements of Japanese society.

The second exhibit depicts the arrival of Commodore Perry in Japan. Perry was nothing for looks but he couldn't have been as ugly and seedy-looking as his wax replica. He is accompanied by two huge, threatening-looking Americans of African ancestry, even though such sailors did not accompany Perry. Poetic license, perhaps?

The rest of the exhibit does not carry such political messages. Most of the models are American movie stars and celebrities. James Dean is loitering in one corner, and Marilyn Monroe is trying to keep her skirt at a modest level in another. The Elvis and Madonna displays are also interesting. The wax museum saves the best for last, with several exhibits showing torture chambers. The Japanese visitors pack these exhibits, as they provide entertainment more vivid than a comic *manga.*

Tokyo Tawa Roningyokan
4-2-8 Shiba Koen, Minato-ku, Tokyo
Tel: 3436-6661

Hours: 10:00–6:00.

Admission: ¥750,
¥400 for children.

CRAFTS

工芸

Building Tool Museum

Toei Shinjuku Line to Morishita Station. Three-minute walk.
See Map 6.

This is the only museum we know of where you should wear a hard hat during your visit. Located in a small lumberyard, the museum is one of the dumpiest we have ever seen. The "curator" had to spend ten minutes moving junk just to let us into the showroom. The collection deserves better, but the surroundings do lend authenticity to the experience.

Japanese houses are traditionally made without a single nail. The joints are assembled like tinker toys, with wooden slats plugged into spaces to provide a secure fit. This method of construction provides excellent protection against earthquakes. The tools that make this possible, and various examples of the finished product, make up the lion's share of the collection.

The curator loved the chance to explain to foreigners the state of the art in Japanese building construction. He is a decent man who knows his job, but he is not a good housekeeper.

Sumida Jutaku Senta Tatemono Dogu Kigumi Shiryokan
1-5-3 Kikugawa, Sumida-ku, Tokyo
Tel: 3633-0328

Hours: 10:00–5:00.
Closed Saturdays and 4th Sunday.   Admission: Free.

Furniture Museum

Bus #5 from Tokyo Station, South Exit, to Harumi Yubinkyokumae, or bus #3 from the South Exit of Shinjuku Station.

This small museum was established in 1972 and, like many boutique museums in Tokyo, it serves a promotional purpose for the company that sponsors it. The museum is located on the second floor of the Japan Interior Center Building. The first floor is crammed with furniture, expensive rugs, and a display room for Knob Hill Furniture imported from the United States. The first floor also has a small cafe where you can quaff complimentary coffee while contemplating your purchase, or plan your decorating scheme with the help of a personal computer. The museum surely lures a few clients in the door.

The museum has more than 1,300 display items but space constraints keep most of them in storage at any given time. English translations are provided for most of the displays, which range from *tansu* (traditional Japanese chests) to Windsor chairs manufactured in colonial America. One of the best items is a beautiful antique medicine chest, handmade in the Chinese style. The medieval Osaka merchant chests are equally remarkable. A series of miniature furniture completes the display.

Kagu no Hakubutsukan
JIC Building, 3-10 Harumi, Chuo-ku, Tokyo
Tel: 3533-0098

Hours: 10:00–4:30.
Closed Wednesday, August 11–17, and December 28–January 5.

Admission: ¥400,
¥200 for 7–18-year-old students.

Glass Book Museum

Sobu Line to Kinshicho Station. Six-minute walk. See Map 6.

The Glass Book Museum is located on the second floor of a new designed-to-look-old building on a street that has attracted a number of immigrants from Thailand. The building houses a small collection of antique glass and trendy modern pieces. Some of the modern pieces are for sale. However, the most remarkable feature of this museum is the fine book collection, located in a small, cheerful room adjacent to the glasswork collection.

Folks interested in the history of glass will have a field day here. The shelves are packed with expensive, coffee-table-type books about stained glass, glassblowing, and related art forms. Most of the books are in English, with a smattering in French, German, and Japanese.

The Glass Book Museum is not far from the Tombstone Museum and the Wood Sculpture Museum, as part of Sumida Ward's "Small Museum Walk." Few foreigners venture into these quarters, and you will be more of a novelty than usual if you grab a map and start museum hunting along this route.

Garasu no Hon no Hakubutsukan
4-10-4 Kinshi, Sumida-ku, Tokyo
Tel: 3625-3755

Hours: 10:00–6:00.
Closed Monday.   Admission: Free.

Japan Folk Crafts Museum

*Inokashira Line from Shibuya to Komaba Todaimae Station.
Ten-minute walk.*

You will see few traditional Japanese residences as spectacular as the one that houses this museum. In keeping with the traditional atmosphere, you remove your shoes and pad through the hallowed halls in slippers.

The museum was established in 1936 with a grant from Magosaburo Ohara, to display folk crafts from Japan, Korea, Taiwan, and Okinawa. Much of the collection consists of handmade clothing, furniture, ceramics, porcelains, and statues from the Edo period when Japan was largely closed to contact with the outside world. It was a time of spectacular cultural achievements.

The museum has two floors, with some of the most beautiful views and displays on the second floor. It is well worth allowing an extra half hour here just to admire the serene beauty of the rooms and the Japanese rock gardens surrounding the building. Take a break, and then continue to wander through rooms displaying clothing suitable for an Utamaro print.

The first floor has a nice gift shop with expensive but beautiful replicas of the displays in the museum. There is a good collection of books and magazines for sale.

Nippon Mingeikan
4-3-33 Komaba, Meguro-ku, Tokyo
Tel: 3467-4527

Hours: 9:00–5:00. Closed Monday
and New Year's Holiday.

Admission: ¥1000,
¥500 for all students.

Kite Museum

Ginza Line to Nihonbashi Station, Exit C7. Two-minute walk,
behind Tokyu Department Store. See Map 1.

This tiny museum is located on the fifth floor of a nondescript building in bustling Nihonbashi. Ride up in the single elevator car, after eyeing the throngs waiting to get into the cheap and excellent Taimeikan Restaurant on the first floor. Bear these crowds in mind as you enter the museum—the former owner of the restaurant used the earnings to fund this museum devoted to his lifelong hobby.

The current curator, Mr. Masaaki Modegi, can be seen making kites in the middle of the museum. Pull up a chair and watch; he is used to visitors. A video display occupies the corner next to the work area, and a mockup of an old Japanese house is on the other side, blending the old and new amid a hodgepodge of weird kites, paper, and junk on the floor.

More than three-thousand kites are crammed into this small room, including tiny kites no bigger than your fingernail, and a big replica of a Japanese Zero Warplane used for target practice during World War II. You can see the entire display in ten minutes, or spend an hour watching a kite being constructed. Be careful when you walk around because it is easy to knock down one of the delicate displays. The next time someone tells you to fly a kite, visit this museum.

Tako no Hakubutsukan
1-12-10 Nihonbashi, Chiyoda-ku, Tokyo
Tel: 3275-2704

Hours: 11:00–5:00.
Closed Sunday.

Admission: ¥300, primary and
middle school students ¥100.

Leather Arts Museum

Ginza Line to Asakusa, Exit 5. Bus #7 to Senju Kiyokawa-Nichome, or Hashiba-Nichome if the bus goes this far. Ten-minute walk from Senju Kiyokawa-Nichome or two-minute walk from Hashiba-Nichome stop. See Map 2.

This is not a museum for sadomasochists; there are no whips here. What you will find is a wonderful and impressive collection of old and new things made from leather. This kind of museum is strange, but its location in Japan is even stranger. During Japan's middle ages, it was considered dirty to handle dead bodies (undertakers and butchers) and the skins of dead animals (tanners and shoemakers). Thus, such jobs were delegated to Japan's lowest caste—the *burakumin*. Even today, the *burakumin* are unmentionables. We found out the hard way that you should not even refer to the *burakumin* in public.

The museum is on two floors of an old grammar school. Ensconced in glass cases, there are antique and new shoes from all over the world including Tanzania, Morocco, China, India, Tibet, America, and Korea. There is also a full-sized set of samurai armor made out of metal and leather. The museum is practically next door to the Japan Toy Museum. Visit both to make your trip complete.

Hikakusangyo Shiryokan
1-36-2 Hashiba, Taito-ku, Tokyo
Tel: 3872-6780

Hours: 10:00–4:00.
Closed Monday.   Admission: Free.

Meiji University Commodity Museum

Hanzomon or Shinjuku Line to Jinbocho Station. Ten-minute walk.
See Map 1.

This colorful museum is one of three free museums located in the same building at Meiji University. The collection is devoted to various Japanese handicrafts including lacquerware, jewelry, crystal, fabric, paper, and pottery.

The exhibits are beautifully presented, even considering the high standards found at most Japanese museums. All exhibits have little drawings depicting how each craft is made, and are accompanied by an English translation.

A visit to Meiji University offers something for every interest. Children may love the Archaeology Museum, men will love the Criminology Museum, and what woman could pass up a chance to visit the Commodity Museum? Even the walk to Meiji University through the nearby Jinbocho neighborhood is interesting. There, you can slurp at some of the best noodle stalls in Japan and browse through the world's largest concentration of bookstores.

Meiji Daigaku Shohin Chinretsukan
1-1 Kanda Surugadai, Chiyoda-ku, Tokyo
Tel: 3296-4433

Hours: 9:30–4:00.
9:30–12:30, Saturday.
Closed Sunday.   Admission: Free.

National Museum of Modern Art Crafts Gallery

Tozai Line to Takebashi Station. Seven-minute walk. Near National Museum of Modern Art.

The old red-brick building looks like it should be on a university campus rather than in a beautiful park in central Tokyo—but who's complaining. The park is fantastic, the building unique, and the collection interesting. Practically all types of Japanese crafts, including pottery, lacquerware, porcelain, and glassware are displayed in illuminated cases. The collection is frequently rotated and temporary exhibits from around the world are exceptional.

The interior has been modified to accommodate the art and has thus lost its charming period decor. At least the old wooden staircase in the foyer was saved. The collection is only on the second floor and the rooms are a bit dark. Opening and closing doors to each room is bothersome and the temperature is a bit hot. Save your ticket and turn it in at the main desk to get a free ticket to the National Museum of Modern Art up the road. The Science Foundation Museum is located in the same park.

Tokyo Kokuritsu Kindai Bijutsukan Kogeikan
1-1 Kitanomaru Koen, Chiyoda-ku, Tokyo
Tel: 3211-7781

Hours: 10:00–5:00.
Closed Monday.

Admission: ¥400, ¥130 for high school and university students, ¥70 for primary and middle school students.

Paper Museum

*Oji Station, South Exit on Keihin Tohoku Line or Oji Station on
Arakawa streetcar. Three-minute walk.*

The Paper Museum, located in the old-fashioned *shitamachi*
or common-people's area of Tokyo, claims to be the only
museum in the world that specializes in paper. The museum
was established in 1950 by what was known as the Oji Paper
Manufacturing Company.

The museum is divided into eight rooms. The first room
has a description of paper manufacturing, and a model of
the first paper-making machine invented by Louis Robert of
France in 1798. The third room has a beautiful collection of
origami, the Japanese art of paper folding. The fourth room
has examples of Egyptian papyrus and Chinese paper from the
Middle Ages. The fifth room is a special display area with an
impressive collection of paper castles, clothing, and dolls from
the *sakoku jidai,* the period from 1611 to 1854, when Japan
was virtually closed to the outside world. The eighth room
provides examples of Japanese paper-making techniques.

The annex has a library of more than seven-thousand
books on paper making and recycling. Virtually all of the
books are in Japanese, and most of the displays do not have
English descriptions. However, videos are shown regularly in
the basement, and are easy to understand.

Kami no Hakubutsukan
1-1-8 Horifune, Kita-ku, Tokyo
Tel: 3911-3545

Hours: 9:30–4:30.
Closed Mondays and national
holidays.

Admission: ¥200,
¥100 for children.

Sasaki Crystal Gallery

Sobu Line to Kinshicho Station. Fifteen-minute walk. See Map 6.

Any lover of fine crystal from around the world will love this museum. The first exhibition room displays vials of multicolored powders which, when heated, produce molten glass. A large replica of a firing oven shows this heating process. The second exhibition room has many showcases containing special glassware from around the world. There are old wood molds used to emboss pressed glass designs. There is even a special set of Baccarat crystal made in 1906 with the Emperor's insignia. The second exhibition room displays glassware from Italy, France, Czechoslovakia, and Sweden. The third exhibition room is almost entirely devoted to Sasaki crystal. A large glass bust of its founder glows in the midday sun. Settings of Sasaki's current product line are artfully displayed for everyday and special occasion use.

Your guide will take you to the third floor where there is an observation deck with a bird's-eye view of the factory. Here you can watch hundreds of workers remove bright-red molten glass from ovens and transform it into translucent stemware. Due to the many tours that are scheduled, you cannot stay for long.

On the fourth floor is a factory outlet store where you can purchase Sasaki glass up to sixty percent off. Be sure to bring plenty of cash.

Sasaki Kurisutaru Gyarari
1-15-2 Yokogawa, Sumida-ku, Tokyo
Tel: 3624-7111

Hours: 9:30–4:30 (by appointment
only). Closed Saturday and Sunday.   Admission: Free.

Silk Museum

Keihin Tohoku Line to Kannai Station. Ten-minute walk.

Men may be bored, but women will love this place. Everything that has to do with silk, from cultivating the silk worms to dyeing those beautiful kimonos, is covered here. If you have always wanted to know how silk thread is made from the cocoons, visit this museum.

The museum provides information about the history of Japan's silk industry. The Japanese boast that they invented the silk scarf. Weaving, dying, and sewing silk is a business but this museum treats the process like it should be treated—as an art. Old looms, kimonos, and theatrical costumes are interesting as are the woodblock prints that show *bijin* (beautiful women) collecting the white silky cocoons. The Yokohama History Archives, the Yokohama Customs Museum, and the Kanagawa Prefecture Museum are nearby—try to see all three.

Siruku Hakubutsukan
1 Yamashitacho, Naka-ku, Yokohama
Tel: 045-641-0841

Hours: 9:00–4:30.
Closed Monday.

Admission: ¥300,
¥200 for university and high school
students, ¥100 for children.

Sword Museum

Odakyu Line from Shinjuku to Sangubashi Station. Ten-minute walk.

The samurai spirit lives on in Yoyogi. The Sword Museum houses a small but good collection of swords and armor from medieval Japan. Before Japan closed its doors shortly after 1600, Japanese swords were exported to Europe and the experts claimed they were better than those made in Toledo, Spain, the standard of excellence in those days.

Don't let such stories of Japanese industrial prowess rankle you, the Japanese also made plenty of lousy swords. Fortunately, the Sword Museum does not deal with such mediocrity. The collection is displayed with the possessions of the Japanese warrior class. Unfortunately, many handles, the most decorative part of the swords, are missing from the main attractions.

Tens of thousands of Japanese swords are held and collected by fans all over the world. The Sword Museum has a disappointingly small collection. If you want to see more, you must go to the annual San Francisco Sword Fair, where wheelers and dealers from Hong Kong to Hamburg gather to augment their collections.

Token Hakubutsukan
4-25-10 Yoyogi, Shibuya-ku, Tokyo
Tel: 3379-1388

Hours: 9:00–4:00.
Closed Monday.

Admission: ¥515,
¥310 for students.

Tombstone Museum

Sobu Line to Kinshicho Station. Seven-minute walk. See Map 6.

The Tombstone Museum may not be the smallest, the weirdest, or the cheeriest museum in Tokyo, but it is one of the hardest to find. Nobody in the neighborhood had heard of it. Shops on either side pointed us in distant directions. Finally, we timidly entered a small shop with a display case on one side and somber gravemarkers on the other. We spotted the museum dead-on!

The proprietor, a shopkeeper seeking a tax advantage by turning his shop into a museum, could not have been more hospitable. He lectured us on gravestone techniques and the best stone to use, "Italian is so expensive we don't deal in it—Swedish granite is the upper end for us." We even left with a sample piece of granite beautifully packaged.

The photos on the wall were mildly interesting—if pictures of quarries from India, the US, and Japan are your cup of tea. There is not much to see in the Tombstone Museum, and the subject matter is a bit depressing, but the proprietor is as kicky and friendly as one of the Grateful Dead.

Sekizai Shiryokan
1-4-10 Kinshi, Sumida-ku, Tokyo
Tel: 3621-3333

Hours: 9:00–5:30.
Closed Wednesday.

Admission: Free.

Woodcrafts Museum

Sobu Line to Ryogoku Station. Six-minute walk. See Map 6.

This museum gives the visitor a great excuse to talk to an old artisan, the sculptor Matsumoto. She also serves as the curator and historian of this museum. Wearing this many hats is easy, she lives upstairs. There are only three display cases, filled with traditional carved wooden panels, decorations, and sculptures. Matsumoto has also carved darling wooden puzzles for children.

This museum is particularly hard to find as the building looks like every other building in the neighborhood. You can feel the collective blood pressure of the locals rise when they realize there are foreigners about. However, Matsumoto is a gracious hostess and is always glad to talk to foreign visitors.

If you are in the area do drop in. The museum is a one-minute walk from the Kanto Earthquake Museum, one of our favorite museums. Don't leave the neighborhood without seeing it.

Mokucho Shiryokan
1-13-3 Ishihara, Sumida-ku, Tokyo
Tel: 3622-4920

Hours: 10:00–4:00.   Admission: Free.

Wood Sculpture Museum

Sobu Line to Kinshicho Station. Eight-minute walk. See Map 6.

When we began writing this book, we were tickled at the thought of visiting museums with weird names. We expected humble "museums" in somebody's garage; instead, we found yuppie art collections in glass and stainless steel homes. The down and dirty eluded us—until we visited this museum.

To visit the Wood Sculpture Museum, you enter a nondescript apartment building and go to the second floor to wake up the "curator." He tells you to go out back, where he lets you into a musty basement packed with his prized collection of sculptures—and broken appliances. You clamber over boxes and other junk while he gives an excited tour of his collection. He is lucky to get three or four visitors per month but this does not dampen his enthusiasm.

The Wood Sculpture Museum may not have much class, but it has a lot of charm. The collection—wooden representations of animals, people, and places—is good enough to warrant better surroundings. For now, you must visit subterranean Sumida Ward, with a gabby curator wiping sleep from his eyes.

Kanso Mokuzai Kogei Shiryokan
2-9-11 Kinshi, Sumida-ku, Tokyo
Tel: 3625-2401

Hours: 10:00–5:00 (reservation calls appreciated). Admission: Free.

HISTORY

歴史

LOCAL

141	Minato Ward Local History Museum	港区立郷土資料館
142	Nakano Ward Historical Museum	山崎記念中野区歴史資料館
143	Ota Ward Folk Museum	大田区立郷土博物館
144	Shinjuku Historical Museum	新宿歴史博物館
145	Suginami Ward Historical Museum	杉並区立郷土博物館
146	Toshima Ward Historical Museum	豊島区立郷土資料館
147	Tsukiji Ward Historical Museum	築地教育会館の郷土資料館
148	Yonbancho Folk Museum	千代田区立四番町歴史民俗資料館

Currency Museum

Ginza Line to Mitsukoshimae Station, Exit A4. Three-minute walk.
Also walking distance from Nihonbashi and Otemachi areas.
See Map 1.

This museum purports to be open by appointment only. When we arrived, the place was jammed with students. The compulsory English-speaking guide, promised when we booked, never materialized. In fact, you don't need to reserve, even though the mavens on the switchboard will insist you do.

Once inside, you can see displays relating to the history of Japanese currency. To some extent, the museum is an inferior rendition of the Ministry of Finance's Printing Museum. The displays at the Currency Museum are decent, but nothing special.

What is a bit special is the *History of Japanese Currency* booklet that is provided gratis to visitors. Written in impeccable English, the booklet gives you the history of the Japanese monetary system in a few pages. Most museums provide handouts, but this is a good one. It compensates for the unremarkable exhibits.

Nihon Ginko Kinyu Kenkyujo Kahei Hakubutsukan
1-3-1 Nihonbashi Hongokucho, Chuo-ku, Tokyo
Tel: 3279-1111

Hours: 9:30–4:30, Monday–Friday.   Admission: Free.

Daimyo Clock Museum

Chiyoda Line to Nezu Station. Seven-minute walk. See Map 2.

The Clock Museum is the product of a private collection created by Guro Kamiguchi, a longtime resident of Taito Ward who developed a fascination with clocks made for the *daimyō* lords of Japan's feudal period. Kamiguchi believed that the pure Japanese-style clocks, created during the period of seclusion, were being bought up by the foreigners at cut-rate prices and that the few Japanese interested in the unique Japanese clocks would be reduced to visiting foreign collections.

Kamiguchi approached antique dealers all over Japan and amassed an impressive collection of medieval Japanese clocks. The collection, now managed by his son, is situated in a large tatami-mat room on beautiful, albeit unkept, grounds owned by the Kamiguchi family. The gardens have tribal art and statues of Buddha lurking in the leaves.

It is worth visiting this museum simply because it forces you to walk the back streets of Nezu, one of the most charming and traditional neighborhoods in the city. Some foreigners call Nezu the "Kyoto of Tokyo," and with good reason. Few neighborhoods offer the peace and old-fashioned atmosphere of Nezu.

Daimyo Tokei Hakubutsukan
2-1-27 Yanaka, Taito-ku, Tokyo
Tel: 3821-6913

Hours: 10:00–4:00.
Closed Monday.
Open January 16 to June 30 and
October 1 to December 24.

Admission: ¥300,
¥200 for children and all students.

Edo-Tokyo Museum

JR Sobu Line to Ryogoku Station. Located next to
Kokugikan Sumo Arena. Three-minute walk.

Just opened as this book was going to press, the Edo-Tokyo Museum is the largest and most ambitious of all the history museums in Tokyo. It is worth the trip just to see the building alone; supported on four massive pillars, it seems to have fallen through a time warp from some future space city.

Inside, life-size reproductions of scenes from Tokyo's past are superbly exhibited in a huge stadium-size room. A reconstruction of the Nihonbashi, Japan's number one bridge, divides the exhibits into two areas: old Edo (as Tokyo was then called) and post-Meiji-Restoration Tokyo. There is a display covering practically every facet of Tokyo's past, from commerce to culture. Particularly fascinating is a replica of Edo's Nakamura-za Kabuki theater, founded in 1624, which during its 270-year history saw Edo Kabuki move away from the style of Kyoto and Osaka and develop its own dynamic plays and scenarios. A mezzanine floor displays a replica of Edo Castle and an intricate model layout of the town.

Wandering around the exhibits, the visitor feels much closer to the past than in conventional history museums where exhibits are shut off behind glass. This feeling is heightened by the frequent demonstrations of traditional folk crafts and art.

If you have time to only visit one history museum in Tokyo, visit this one.

Tokyo-to Edo Tokyo Hakubutsukan
1-4-1 Yokoami, Sumida-ku, Tokyo
Tel: 3626-8000

Hours: 10:00–6:00. Friday 10:00–9:00. Closed Monday (unless it is a national holiday, then closed Tuesday).

Admission: ¥500, high school students and under, ¥250.

105

Fisherman's Culture Museum

Marunouchi Line to Yotsuya-Sanchome Station. Five-minute walk.
See Map 5.

This museum is located next to an office that publishes a fisherman's newspaper. To enter, you must go into the newspaper office, where an editor will grab a key, turn on the lights, and give you a tour of the large collection of items memorializing the history of fishing in Japan. The museum has a large collection of fishing rods, ancient and new. Our guide lamented the passing of the old traditions, "These new kids never use bamboo rods." The really old traditions are preserved in a special exhibit showing old fishing tackle from China. The early Japanese equipment appears to have been closely patterned after the Chinese originals.

The thought of fresh, raw fish makes the Japanese heart race, and this enthusiasm carries over to the men who stand guard over the Fisherman's Culture Museum. They love fishing, and can't understand when foreign visitors say they don't fish, they just like museums.

Tsuri Bunka Shiryokan
18-7 Aizumicho, Shinjuku-ku, Tokyo
Tel: 3355-6242

Hours: 10:00–5:00, Monday–
Friday.
2nd and 3rd Saturdays, 10:00–3:00.   Admission: Free.

Fukagawa Edo Museum

Tozai Line to Monzen-Nakacho Station. Fifteen-minute walk, or take the local bus to the museum.

Each year, millions of foreign visitors come to Japan expecting to see women in kimonos, a tea ceremony, and woodblock prints. Instead, the visitors see the intense concrete jungle of Tokyo. These visitors are disappointed that they have missed the old Japan.

The old Japan may only exist in memories, but at least there is a magnificent museum to document Japan's glorious past. The Fukagawa Edo Museum has a huge room with a life-size replica of a seventeenth-century Tokyo neighborhood. The Edo Museum is quite authentic, as you will see by the laundry hanging from the eaves, stone sidewalks, and tiny marina. This is how Tokyo looked during Japan's period of seclusion.

There are so many thoughtful details in the museum. If you allow enough time, you can see the village by night: the ceiling skylights periodically fold up and arc lights are turned on. The atmosphere lasts for an hour or so, and daybreak comes again.

Be sure to take your shoes off and explore the interior of some of the buildings. Each room has something different. Children will enjoy playing with the toys, while others will enjoy the parlors and kitchens of the medieval city. The video programs are quite interesting.

Fukagawa Edo Shiryokan
1-3-28 Shirakawa, Koto-ku, Tokyo
Tel: 3630-8625

Hours: 10:00–4:30.

Admission: ¥300,
¥50 for children.

107

Igusa Hachimangu Folklore Collection

Marunouchi Line or JR Sobu Line to Ogikubo Station, ten-minute bus ride to Hachimangu-ura. Three-minute walk.

This museum is more like a musty old antique shop than a proper museum. It occupies a small room at the back of the beautiful Hachimangu Shrine complex. The museum was established forty years ago, and has gradually acquired a diverse folklore collection. The collection consists of old tools and appliances used in Japan in the nineteenth century.

You can try using a wooden rice-hulling machine and other tools used in processing traditional Japanese food. An even mustier room in the back contains a replica of an old Japanese kitchen. The walls are crammed with junk, adding authenticity to the experience. Old toys, saké bottles, and musical instruments round out the collection.

This is not a fancy museum, but it is a charming experience to poke around the place, something like going through someone's attic. The proud curator, Mr. Sekine, is as polite and enthusiastic as can be. He gets few foreign visitors, and is delighted to show such visitors the rudiments of old Japan that have accumulated in his presence.

Igusa Hachimangu Shiryokan
1-33-1 Zenpukuji, Suginami-ku, Tokyo
Tel: 3399-8133

Hours: 10:00–3:00 (open only on
1st Sunday of the month).

Admission: ¥200,
¥100 for children.

Japanese War-Dead Memorial Museum

Subway to Kudanshita Station, Exit 2. Eight-minute walk.
See Map 1.

Visiting this museum is almost as spooky as going to the Kanto Earthquake Museum. The Yushukan is located in the grounds of the Yasukuni Shrine, one of the most important Shinto shrines in Japan. However, the Yasukuni Shrine has a special political significance that transcends its Shinto origins: it is the Japanese Bittburg. The names of Hideki Tojo, and six other Class A war criminals who were executed by the Allied war tribunal or committed suicide, are honored here. Former prime minister, Yasuhiro Nakasone, caused a furor by visiting here.

The museum has many mementos of World War II, including a lifesize Zero fighter plane and a mockup of an aircraft carrier. The famous kamikaze as well as medical personnel are also honored. Smaller rooms house hard-to-swallow displays glorifying the activities of the Japanese army in China, Malaya, and elsewhere. Definitely worth the time is a thirty-minute video about the life of the current emperor. The film is surprisingly even-handed, given the sensitive position of the royal family. Rare footage of the royal family, backed by music by the American composer Samuel Barber, leaves a lasting impression on the Western visitor.

Yushukan
3-1-1 Kudan-Kita, Chiyoda-ku, Tokyo
Tel: 3261-8326

Admission: ¥200,
¥50 for primary school students.

Hours: 9:00–4:30.

109

Kagawa Archives and Resource Center

Keio Line to Kami-Kitazawa Station. Two-minute walk.

Toyohiko Kagawa is almost forgotten today, but he was a famous person in the postwar era. Some commentators called him the Japanese Gandhi, or the St. Francis of the twentieth century. Kagawa, like so many famous Japanese, was born as the illegitimate son of a rich man. He converted to Christianity at the age of fifteen. He studied at the Princeton Theological Seminary, but didn't let the wanton ways of the fraternity boys go to his head.

During his life he was an ardent supporter of human rights and devoted his life to the less fortunate. He rebuilt his congregation after the Great Kanto Earthquake in 1923. When he saw that Japan and the US were headed for war, he bought a ticket to the US and gave impassioned speeches all over the country. He went into hiding from the Thought Police upon his return to Japan, and survived.

Visit this museum. The little chapel has speakers broadcasting his sermons to the empty pews. It is a nostalgic experience.

Kagawa Toyohiko Kinen Matsuzawa Shiryokan
3-8-19 Kami-Kitazawa, Setagaya-ku, Tokyo
Tel: 3302-2855

Hours: 10:00–4:30, Tuesday–Saturday. 1:00–4:00 on Sunday.

Admission: ¥300, ¥200 for high, middle, and primary school students.

Kanto Earthquake Memorial Museum

JR Sobu Line to Ryogoku Station. Ten-minute walk past the Ryogoku Kokugikan (Sumo Stadium). See Map 6.

When you approach this museum, you may get a lump in your throat; not only because the museum memorializes the 140,000 people killed in the Great Kanto Earthquake of September 1, 1923, but because you know that Tokyo is due for another big earthquake. When it happens, you will be glad that you visited this museum.

The first floor describes the earthquake and the disastrous fire that raged for thirty hours after the 8.2 Richter-scale quake. You will see metal appliances melted by the blaze, and a fascinating series of charts showing the hardest hit areas of Tokyo. We found no reference to the massacre by police and vigilantes of at least four-thousand Korean residents of Tokyo, who were blamed for the quake and the fire, and subject to bogus claims of "sabotage," such as the poisoning of wells.

The second floor has displays providing historical information, including charts documenting the incidence and intensity of Tokyo-area quakes over the last two thousand years. The final display depicts the worldwide relief effort organized in the aftermath of the quake.

Tokyo-to Fudo Kinenkan
2-3-25 Yokoami, Sumida-ku, Tokyo
Tel: 3623-1200

Hours: 9:00–5:00. Closed Monday.   Admission: Free.

111

Kasei University Living History Museum

Saikyo Line from Shinjuku or Ikebukuro to Jujo Station. Seven-minute walk.

This museum is dedicated to the lifestyle of university students at Tokyo Kasei University. The collection is spread over two floors of the university's main building, and includes old tools, costumes, and memorabilia from days past. Such nostalgic collections are not unusual in Tokyo, but this one is still worth a visit. No other museum in Tokyo focuses on student memorabilia, and several displays are worth the effort to get here.

We never knew that each prefecture in Japan has its own special sushi. This museum has wax models of local sushi. Chiba Prefecture has the prettiest sushi; Kagoshima Prefecture, the most exotic. The museum also has wax models of typical meals eaten during the different eras of Japanese history. Serving techniques for *soba* and *udon* dishes have changed very little over the last four hundred years.

The friendly curator speaks a little English and will point out the miniature clothes and traditional kimonos. Do not spend all your time on the fourth floor and forget to visit the third floor. An excellent collection of Japanese dolls fills an entire room.

Tokyo-to Kasei Daigaku Seikatsu Shiryokan
1-18-1 Kaga, Itabashi-ku, Tokyo
Tel: 3961-5226

Hours: 9:30–4:00, Monday–Friday.
9:30–11:00 on Saturday.   Admission: Free.

Kokugakuin University Shinto Museum

Bus #3 from Shibuya Station to Kokugakuin Daigakumae Station. One-minute walk. See Map 4.

Shinto is the old tribal religion of Japan. In most other societies, nature cults such as Shinto have given way to other religions. In Japan, Shinto coexists with many forms of Buddhism. Many Japanese get married in Shinto shrines and have funeral services in Buddhist temples.

The Shinto Museum of Kokugakuin University is a small cache of Shinto culture. The museum is in a dark room, adjacent to the cluttered office of a Shinto scholar. Glass cases preserve the ceremonial garb of Shinto shamans. Detailed explanations of Shinto traditions and rites are provided for people literate in the Japanese language. However, the collection is small and can be seen in a few minutes.

Kokugakuin University has a very peaceful atmosphere and many museums within the confines of its campus. The Shinto Museum itself hardly warrants an independent visit, but Kokugakuin University does.

Kokugakuin Daigaku Shinto Shiryokan
4-10-28 Higashi, Shibuya-ku, Tokyo
Tel: 5466-0111 (ask for the extension for the Shinto Shiryokan)

Hours:
Monday and Friday 10:30–3:30,
Wednesday 10:30–6:00.
Admission at other times upon
request to the curator.   Admission: Free.

113

Lucky Dragon Memorial

*Yurakucho Line to Shin-Kiba. Located inside the Yumenoshima Park
near the Tropical Plant Dome. Seven-minute walk.*

On March 4, 1954, the US exploded a hydrogen bomb at
Bikini Atoll. The explosion was more powerful than the
Americans thought; fallout from the blast contaminated both
American troops and Pacific islanders.

About 160 kilometers away, twenty-three Japanese fishermen on the Lucky Dragon V were contaminated by the fallout. Six of the crewmen died during the next thirty-five
years. Japan angrily denied the US charge that the fishermen
were spying on the experiment. The tragedy would have been
largely forgotten, along with other maritime disasters of
the period, if the Peace Society of the Lucky Dragon had not
built a spectacular museum to house the ship and the crew's
mementos in Koto Ward.

Western visitors should be prepared for some hateful
glances. The displays are shrill in their criticism of the US, and
scarcely mention the US apology, payment of compensation,
and the licensing of US nuclear technology to Japan free of
charge, which Japan eagerly accepted. The controversy con-
tinues to rage; we saw three national television programs on
the incident while we were writing this book.

Daigo Fukuryu Maru Kinenkan
3-2 Yumenoshima, Koto-ku, Tokyo
Tel: 3521-8494

Hours: 9:30–4:00.   Admission: Free.
Closed Monday.

Map Museum

Shinjuku, Tozai, or Hanzomon Line to Kudanshita Station, Exit 2.
Four-minute walk. See Map 1.

This museum is located in a grand stone building, around the corner from the Indian Embassy, next door to the Italian Culture Center and within walking distance of the Yasukuni Shrine. The collection spans two floors, and it is unlike anything else in Tokyo. Ninety percent of the exhibits are maps of old Tokyo.

Anyone with a taste for history will like these weird old maps. Some are done in the same fashion as woodblock prints; others are done in a more modern, twentieth-century style. All of them give you an idea of what the streets of old Edo must have looked like.

A visitor to the museum may wonder why modern Tokyo's layout reverted to the incomprehensible format that prevailed prior to the Great Kanto Earthquake and fire of September 1, 1923. Other cities took the opportunity created by catastrophic fires to rebuild in an orderly grid pattern. Even Kyoto opted for this design after architects visited the orderly Chinese city of Changan in the ninth century. Tokyo rebuilt in the old fashion, causing cabdrivers consternation—until the next earthquake and fire burns out the streets too crooked to drive on.

Senshu Bunko
2-1-36 Kudan-Minami, Chiyoda-ku, Tokyo
Tel: 3261-0075

Hours: 10:00–4:00.
Closed Sunday.

Admission: ¥300,
¥200 for university and high school students, ¥150 for middle and primary school students.

115

Meiji Shrine Memorial Picture Gallery

Sobu Line to Shinanomachi Station. Five-minute walk.

This impressive building commemorates one of the greatest figures in Japanese history—the Emperor Meiji, who lived from 1852 to 1912, ruling during the period when Japan was transformed from a hermit nation to one of the most influential nations on earth. The austere exterior will surprise you; the inside is a wonderful blend of art-deco furnishings with mahogany paneling.

The collection includes forty huge paintings depicting the life of the emperor. The most interesting paintings deal with his early life, and the mysterious court customs of the Japanese royal family. The best artists in Japan were commissioned to create these paintings. Some are excellent, but most fall into a uniform pattern of artistic imitation.

Many of the sensitive issues in Japanese history are sugar-coated beyond belief. Korean visitors may be surprised to read that, in 1910, Japan sent a representative to Korea to restore order. The descriptions of the circumstances surrounding the Russo-Japanese War and the occupation of Taiwan are just as incredible.

There are many interesting things to see around this museum. The National Sports Stadium and the Meiji Shrine are nearby.

Meiji Jingu Seitoku Kinen Kaigakan
9 Kasumigaoka, Shinjuku-ku, Tokyo
Tel: 3401-5179

Admission: ¥300, ¥250 for students.

Hours: 9:00–4:00.

Meiji University Criminological Museum

Hanzomon or Shinjuku Line to Jinbocho Station. Ten-minute walk.
See Map 1.

This museum is one of three museums located in the same building at Meiji University. All are free and all are interesting. The Criminological Museum depicts the history of crime and punishment in Japan. The museum displays numerous wood-block prints showing early Japanese criminals and how they were punished. Instruments of torture, including huge torture racks, are also displayed. This is evidently how the subject matter of *manga*, Japan's lurid comic books, got its start. The museum shows the transformation of Japan from a dangerous nation to one of the world's safest. Old police uniforms and memorabilia also round out the collection.

A visit to this museum can be a bit spooky. There is no ticket control—you just walk in after getting off the elevator. The museum also has very few visitors so there is a good chance that you will have the exhibits to yourself.

You should visit all three Meiji museums, as well as explore the interesting Jinbocho area surrounding the university. Few day excursions in Japan are as cheap or interesting.

Meiji Daigaku Keiji Hakubutsukan
1-1 Kanda Surugadai, Chiyoda-ku, Tokyo
Tel: 3296-4431

Hours: 9:00–4:30.
9:00–12:30, Saturday.   Admission: Free.
Closed Sunday.

117

Naruse Memorial Hall

Yamanote Line to Mejiro Station. Fifteen-minute walk.

A son of a samurai of the Choshu clan, Jinzo Naruse was born in June of 1858. Despite his macho gene pool, Naruse was one of the leading advocates of women's education. Considering the era and the cultural mores of early twentieth-century Japan, he was indeed an insightful man. In 1901, Japan Women's University was founded "to educate women as human beings." The spanking-new memorial hall displays mementos of Naruse's life including his scholarly books, articles, and poetry. The grand staircase leading to the second floor is accented with a vaulted ceiling and stained-glass window. However, the collection of artifacts does little justice to the achievements of this great man.

Naruse converted to Christianity in 1877 and traveled to the United States in 1890, where he attended Andover Theological Seminary and Clark University. In 1912 he organized the Concordia Association and met India's Sir Rabindranath Tagore in 1916. Naruse died from liver cancer in 1919.

The museum is within walking distance of the Eisei Bunko and Music Box museums.

Naruse Kinenkan
2-8-1 Mejirodai, Bunkyo-ku, Tokyo
Tel: 3943-3131

Hours: 9:30–4:30, Tuesday–Friday.
9:30–12:00, Saturday.   Admission: Free.

National Museum of Japanese History

Keisei Line to Sakura Station. Ten-minute walk.

Every year, millions of people zip to and from Narita Airport without realizing that they pass close by one of the best historical museums in Japan. It costs little to break your trip to Narita with a stopover in Sakura, and a visit to this museum, and the nearby Kawamura Museum, would be the perfect way to spend a short layover at Narita.

The collection is huge and covers every era in Japanese history. The extensive display on the evolution of domestic travel in Japan is particularly interesting. Another charming detail is the collection of original books about Japan that were published in Europe two or three hundred years ago. However, you can only view them under glass.

The museum is surrounded by a large park. The air quality in Chiba is substantially better than Tokyo's, and the place is peaceful enough to warrant a long walk.

Kokuritsu Rekishi Hakubutsukan
117 Jonaicho, Sakura-shi, Chiba 285
Tel: 0434-86-0123

Admission: ¥400, ¥250 for university and high school students, ¥110 for primary and middle school students.

Hours: 9:30–4:30.

119

Noguchi Museum

Marunouchi Line to Yotsuya-Sanchome Station, Exit 1. Eight-minute walk. See Map 5.

Hideyo Noguchi was as handsome and brilliant a scientist as Japan has produced. Noguchi was born in 1876 and lost all of the fingers on his left hand due to a burn injury and unsuccessful surgery. The young boy studied hard to become a doctor so that he could prevent such tragedies. His efforts are still reverberating in the medical world.

He studied at the University of Pennsylvania and the Rockefeller Medical Research Institute, and was instrumental in advancing research in diseases such as rabies, yellow fever, and cholera.

Noguchi's research took him all over the globe. Many historians credit him with averting a yellow-fever epidemic in Guayaquil, Ecuador in 1919. Noguchi may have won the Nobel Prize in Medicine if he had rested on his laurels, living with his American wife Mary at their home in upstate New York. Instead, he went to West Africa to avert another yellow-fever epidemic. He died while still there.

All this boils down to a weird little room that foreigners never visit. His birthplace and final African dwelling are represented by small models in the left corner of the entrance. His uniforms, papers, and memorabilia are sprawled around the rest of the room. It is a strange and fascinating place to visit.

Noguchi Hideyo Kinenkan
26 Daikyocho, Shinjuku-ku, Tokyo
Tel: 3357-0741

Hours: 9:00–5:00, Monday–Friday.
9:00–3:00, Saturday.   Admission: Free.

Yumenoshima Tropical Plant Dome

Yokohama Maritime Museum

Tokyo Electric
Service Center

Sogakudo Museum

Kanagawa Prefectural Museum

Hayashi Memorial Hall

Kokugakuin University Shinto Museum

Kagawa Archives and Resource Center

Ace World-Bag Museum

Kite Museum

Asakura Choso Museum
photograph by Jude Brand

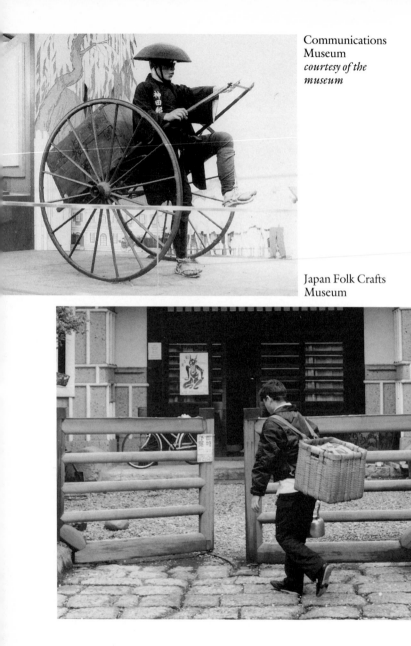

Communications
Museum
*courtesy of the
museum*

Japan Folk Crafts
Museum

Ozaki Memorial Museum

Yurakucho Line to Nagatacho Station, Exit 2. Three-minute walk.
See Map 1.

This museum was opened in 1960, in memory of one of Japan's most illustrious politicians. Ozaki was successful in twenty-five consecutive elections, a world record, and served as a member of the Diet for sixty-three years.

However, Ozaki's career was distinguished by factors greater than longevity. Throughout his career he stood for democratic principles. He endangered his career and his life by speaking out against the militarists who seized control of Japan prior to World War II.

Ozaki was also responsible for the annual cherry blossom festival in Washington D.C. In 1912, Ozaki learned that Mrs. Taft greatly admired Japanese cherry blossom trees. Ozaki had long advocated a symbolic act of gratitude to the United States for its crucial assistance to Japan during the Russo-Japanese War. He defied the government and arranged for the shipment of three thousand cherry blossom trees to Washington D.C.

The memorial is filled with personal mementoes of Ozaki's life, including gifts from many famous world leaders. Paintings of Abraham Lincoln and other Ozaki heroes adorn the walls.

Ozaki Yukio Kinenkan
1-1-1 Nagatacho, Chiyoda-ku, Tokyo
Tel: 3581-1778

Hours: 9:30–4:30.
Closed Saturday and Sunday.   Admission: Free.

Parliamentary Museum

Yurakucho Line to Nagatacho Station, Exit 2. Three-minute walk.
See Map 1.

The Parliamentary Muscum was completed in 1972 to commemorate the National Diet of Japan. With a total floor space of 5,300 meters, it is one of Japan's grander political museums. The site of the museum represents ground zero in Japan. A stone structure in the north garden, installed in 1891, is still used as the basis for surveying the country. The second floor has the best exhibits, including a model of the chamber of the House of Representatives and replicas of the overstuffed chairs where the politicians sit.

Diet sessions are often televised in Japan, and sometimes seem like a genteel form of bear-baiting. The normally polite Japanese yell, call each other names, and take part in an occasional fistfight. After seeing some of this mayhem on television, it is a bit surprising to see the prim and proper museum, with facts and figures strong.

The first floor of the Parliamentary Museum houses the Ozaki Memorial Hall, commemorating one of Japan's most famous politicians. By all means visit both museums.

Kensei Kinenkan
1-1-1 Nagatacho, Chiyoda-ku, Tokyo
Tel: 3581-1178

Hours: 9:30–4:30.
Closed Saturday and Sunday.   Admission: Free.

Printing Bureau Museum

JR or Yurakucho Line to Ichigaya Station. Fifteen-minute walk.

This museum is administered by the Ministry of Finance, and commemorates the history of paper money and stamps in Japan. The exhibits are new and appealing to the eye. No other museum in Tokyo provides as much English language explanation. There are bilingual video terminals where you can select short tapes on various topics regarding the history, production, and collection of stamps and currency. Don't miss the one describing the luminaries on the one, five, and ten-thousand yen notes. Other first floor displays depict how Japan acquired advanced printing technology from Europe and the US, and applied it to Japan's stamps and money. Unfortunately they don't give out free samples.

The second floor is more somber, with displays of old Japanese and foreign stamps, and paper money. The atmosphere is a bit austere compared to the cheerful first floor. A good, cheap restaurant with bar and large television occupies the remainder of the second floor.

Insatsu-kyoku Kinenkan
9-5 Honmuracho, Shinjuku-ku, Tokyo
Tel: 3268-3271

Hours: 9:30–4:30.
Closed Monday.   Admission: Free.

Shaving Culture Museum

Chiyoda Line to Meiji Jingumae Station, Exit A3. Four-minute walk.
See Map 4.

Here you can get shaved and it doesn't cost you two bits. After you do a quick course in shaving history, you can step up to one of the three vanities and shave away with the latest technology in wet shaving. The museum is open until six—awaiting your five o'clock shadow. A free sample of the newest razor is sometimes provided.

This museum was much larger when it opened in 1990 and was solely devoted to the historical aspects of shaving. However, as visitors saw the beautiful old-fashioned straight edges, shaving cups, and soft brushes, a demand for classic shaving instruments resulted. The owner, Mr. Takeuchi, a long time distributor of beard busters in Japan, accommodated the public by stocking high-end shaving equipment in the museum. As sales increased the museum space decreased.

However, the interesting display of the stone-age blades, sixth-century Asian scalp razors, the 1960s safety razors, and the ejectable razors, makes you thankful shaving is now a relatively safe procedure. You won't find any electric razors in this place.

This museum is located only a few minutes away from the Ota Museum and the Do! Family Art Museum.

Kamisori Kurabu
1-14-12 Jingumae, Shibuya-ku, Tokyo
Tel: 5474-0250

Hours: 10:30–6:30.
Closed Sunday.   Admission: Free.

Shitamachi Museum

Yamanote Line to Ueno Station. Five-minute walk. See Map 2.

This is a rarity, a Tokyo museum that does not live up to its potential. The Shitamachi Museum is dedicated to the old days in Tokyo, and promises a charming replica of an old Tokyo street. The idea would be delightful if properly developed like the Fukagawa Edo Museum.

However, this museum is simply too small to do justice to the concept. The old street on display is tiny and rather gloomy. Other displays are more interesting, but space is limited. Surely *shitamachi* deserves better, after all this area is one of the main repositories of old Tokyo. The people of *shitamachi* are the cockneys of Tokyo, and are considered to be traditional, conservative, and even a little backward. If Archie Bunker lived in Tokyo, he would live in *shitamachi*.

Unfortunately, the Shitamachi Museum does not have enough space or resources to replicate old Tokyo. If you are day-tripping in Ueno Park, and are tired of the crowds and the glitzy museums, you might enjoy the Shitamachi Museum. However, if you want to see what old Tokyo looked like, go to the Fukagawa Edo Museum.

Taito Kuritsu Shitamachi Fuzoku Shiryokan
2-1 Ueno Koen, Taito-ku, Tokyo
Tel: 3823-7451

Hours: 9:30–4:30.
Closed Monday.   Admission: ¥200.

125

Shibusawa Memorial Museum

Nanboku Line to Nishigahara Station, Exit 2. Eight-minute walk.

The lawn may need watering and the tables a good dusting, but otherwise it is hard to find fault with this rarely-visited museum in northern Tokyo. Viscount Shibusawa, one of the founders of the Dai-Ichi Kangyo Bank, resided here during the last years of his life. The mansion and grounds have the atmosphere of European royalty.

The first floor contains Shibusawa memorabilia. Shibusawa was a genuine internationalist, and proudly displayed letters from Thomas Edison and other turn-of-the-century luminaries. The Viscount's book collection occupies one wall, also in need of a good dusting.

Allow yourself enough time to walk around the spacious grounds. Even the servants' quarters are lavish. Most estates-turned museum have a manicured quality that the Shibusawa estate obviously lacks, but that adds to the charm and authenticity of the experience.

Shibusawa Shiryokan
2-16-1 Nishigahara, Kita-ku, Tokyo
Tel: 3910-0005

Hours: 10:00–4:00.
Closed Sunday.   Admission: ¥200.

Stationery Museum

Sobu Line to Asakusabashi. Two-minute walk. See Map 1.

The Japanese writing system requires great precision in writing. A person's status is sometimes judged by how well he or she can write *kanji* (Chinese characters). It is not surprising that Japan has a highly developed system of writing implements. The Stationery Museum gives you a glimpse of this phenomenon.

Looking at Japanese writing implements makes you wonder if studying calligraphy may be as much of a seemingly hopeless cause as studying Japanese. A decent calligraphy set seems to encompass a dizzying variety of brushes, ink, and supporting tools.

This museum has a good collection of European and American pens, from Parker to da Vinci. The old posters advertising fountain pens are very interesting, as are the posters depicting the evolution of writing instruments from the Egyptians to the present.

Each visitor who signs the guest book receives a free ballpoint pen. Unfortunately, the pen we received did not work.

Bungu Shiryokan
1-1-15 Yanagibashi, Taito-ku, Tokyo
Tel: 3861-4905

Hours: 10:00–4:00, Monday–
Friday.   Admission: Free.

Stock Market Museum

Tozai Line to Kayabacho Station. Four-minute walk. See Map 1.

During the 1980s, the Tokyo Stock Exchange became famous as the site of the biggest speculative explosion in world history. The Nikkei index swooned in the early 1990s, but the Tokyo Stock Market is likely to remain near the top of the financial heap well into the twenty-first century.

You can combine a visit to the museum with a tour of the visitors' gallery of the exchange. This allows you to observe the frantic traders as they scurry around the trading floor. The thick glass windows enable you to see but not hear the commotion down below. The tour that includes the visitors' gallery is more interesting than the museum, but you can soak up some history by visiting the museum as well.

The collection includes photos, stock certificates, and illustrations of the early days of the exchange. Charts and graphs proudly trace the speculative bubble to its peak on the last trading day of 1989. The recurrent insider-trading scandals that rocked the exchange in 1991 are ignored.

Kabutocho Hakubutsukan
2-1 Nihonbashi, Kabutocho, Chuo-ku, Tokyo
Tel: 3666-0141

Hours: 9:00–4:00.
Closed Saturday and Sunday.   Admission: Free.

Tobacco and Salt Museum

*Yamanote Line to Shibuya Station. Ten-minute walk from the station.
See Map 4.*

You don't have to be a hard-core smoker to enjoy this place. The museum is housed in a bright new building in trendy Shibuya, and covers four floors.

The first floor houses the information desk, shop, and audio-visual lecture hall. Tobacco products are also sold at a small store. The second floor traces the "Route of Tobacco" from its origins in Bolivia and Argentina, to the rest of the world. There are several self-starting video displays and a huge globe tracing the path of the tobacco trade. An intermediate floor, branded "2f," features the history of Japanese tobacco. This floor is packed with everything from woodblock prints to high-tech video displays depicting cigarette manufacturing.

The third floor is a combination exhibit, showing the history of foreign and Japanese salt. This intermingling of foreign displays and unique Japanese displays has not diluted the cachet of the exhibit, as you can see salt mines and mockups of old Japanese salt production.

The fourth floor is given over to traveling exhibits. As is the case with many museums, these can be the best or the worst exhibitions in the entire building. Our visit found a fantastic display about Dutch Nagasaki, including weird woodblocks and a replica of Dejima Island.

Tabako to Shio no Hakubutsukan
1-16-8 Jinnan, Shibuya-ku, Tokyo
Tel: 3476-2041

Hours: 10:00–6:00. Closed Monday.

Admission: ¥100, ¥50 for children
and high school students.

Toraya Museum

Marunouchi or Ginza Line to Akasaka Mitsuke Station. Seven-minute walk. See Map 1.

When you see old ladies pushing their way onto Tokyo subway trains, they are often carrying little black bags with a golden, three-lion logo. The bags contain *yōkan* (Japanese bean sweets), and the bags come from the company that runs this museum.

The first floor has a nice shop selling high-priced sweets in beautiful boxes. The second floor has a little museum showing the evolution of unique Japanese sweets. Japanese children salivate over this stuff, but foreigners normally prefer chocolate.

The museum is located near the wonderful Akasaka neighborhood, and is within walking distance of the Sogetsu Museum (modern art) and the Suntory Museum (culture-vulture heaven).

Toraya Bunko
4-9-22 Akasaka, Minato-ku, Tokyo
Tel: 3408-2402

Hours: 10:00–5:00, Monday–
Friday.
Also closed at irregular intervals.
Phone to confirm.   Admission: Free.

Tsubouchi Theater Museum

Tozai Line to Waseda Station. Twelve-minute walk. See Map 5.

This museum is located within the walls of Waseda University and is dedicated to Dr. Tsubouchi, the man who translated all of Shakespeare's works into Japanese. The museum building, completed in 1928, is modeled after London's Fortune Theatre, and has been lovingly restored. Even if you don't care about theater, you will love the building. It is a bit of Elizabethan England in the middle of Tokyo. The wooden floors, archways, and quaint fixtures add to the old atmosphere.

The collection occupies the second and third floors of the building, and spans Western and Japanese theatrical arts. There are numerous models of Japanese and Western stages, as well as costumes, masks, and props. The porch of the building represents the stage of an Elizabethan theater, and has been the site of theatrical performances.

The Waseda University area is very lively. You can combine a visit to this museum with a ride on Tokyo's last streetcar, the *chin-chin densha*, which begins in front of Waseda's campus walls. The trolley car is the best way to visit the Paper Museum. Visit both in the same day and experience Japanese campus life at the same time.

Tsubouchi Hakubutsukan
1-6-1 Nishi-Waseda, Shinjuku-ku, Tokyo
Tel: 3203-4141

Hours: 9:00–5:00. Closed Monday.
Open April 1 to July 31, and
mid-September to March 31.   Admission: Free.

Yamate Museum

Bus #11 from Sakuragicho Station. Two-minute walk.

This museum has one of the best locations in Yokohama. It is located on a bluff overlooking the city near the popular tourist destination, the Foreigners' Cemetery (only in Japan would looking at dead foreigners become a tourist attraction).

The museum is located in a reconstructed relic of the time when the Yamate neighborhood was a foreign enclave in Yokohama. The house is beautiful, but always seems to be under renovation.

The collection includes photos and memorabilia of the late nineteenth century, when a tiny, English-speaking foreign community conducted trade between Japan and the outside world. The collection is not much, but the neighborhood has considerable historical significance and many things to see. Many Japanese consider it to be an exotic experience to see the Western-style buildings and crucifixes on tombstones. It may not be as exotic for Western visitors, but it is a worthwhile day-trip out of Tokyo.

Yamate Shiryokan
247 Yamatecho, Naka-ku, Yokohama
Tel: 045-622-1188

Hours: 11:00–4:00.
Call before a Sunday visit.   Admission: Free.

Yokohama Customs Museum

Keihin Tohoku Line to Kannai Station. Fifteen-minute walk.

If you want to see how the ever-alert Port Customs Authority spots contraband bound for Japan, this is the place for you. Located in an old building typical of Yokohama's business district, the museum dwells on displays of foiled smuggling attempts.

The featured items include illicit drugs, precious metals, and guns secreted away in false tables, platform shoes, and ceramic statues. Hopefully, visitors won't get any ideas. The displays of fake handbags, polo shirts, and perfumes remind you not to bring back designer apparel bought at rock-bottom prices at South Asian market stalls. The remaining displays are interesting and inform the visitor of the rough-and-ready days of early Yokohama.

Yokohama Zeikan Tenjishitsu
1-1 Kaigan-dori, Naka-ku, Yokohama
Tel: 045-212-6010

Hours: 10:00–4:00.
Closed Saturday and Sunday.

Admission: Free.

Yokohama History Archives

Keihin Tohoku Line to Kannai Station. Ten-minute walk.

In 1854, Commodore Perry signed the first treaty between the US and Japan underneath a camphor tree near the harbor in Yokohama. The ceremony followed a demonstration of a small train set and a wireless machine brought by Perry as gifts to Japan. The ceremony marked the end of 250 years of Japan's isolation from Western nations.

The camphor tree burned down during the catastrophic fire that raged after the Great Kanto Earthquake in 1923, but the roots survived. Japanese gardeners nursed the tree back to life, and it now occupies a courtyard in the fascinating Yokohama History Archives.

The first floor of the museum could be termed the "Black Ships Gallery," because it has the most detailed description in Japan of Perry's visit. The most interesting items are enlargements of English newspaper articles from the period describing Perry's visit. The second floor is packed with interesting exhibits documenting Yokohama's role in the early years of trade with the US and Europe. All in all, this is one of the best historical museums in the Tokyo Metropolitan area.

Yokohama Kaiko Shiryokan
3 Nihon-Odori, Naka-ku, Yokohama
Tel: 045-201-2100

Hours: 9:30–5:00.
Closed Monday.

Admission: ¥200,
¥100 for children, primary, and
middle school students.

134

Adachi Ward Museum

*Bus #28 from Chiyoda Line Kameari Station to Hakubutsukan-mae
(near Oyata-Gochome). One-minute walk.*

A bit off the beaten path, Adachi Ward is located in northern Tokyo. About five-thousand years ago Adachi Ward was actually the bottom of the sea, and the locals are quite proud of this bit of history. The museum is new and spacious and contains the typical displays found in other local ward museums including an Edo house, old Buddha statues, and broken pottery. The wing devoted to woodblock prints is wonderful and the toy case upstairs colorful.

　　The garden out back is beautiful and has a tea house which can be rented out for private parties at a "minimal cost." If you want to see a nice museum that is not crowded, spend the afternoon wandering the gardens on the ocean floor.

Adachi Kuritsu Kyodo Hakubutsukan
5-20-1 Oyata, Adachi-ku, Tokyo
Tel: 3620-9393

Hours: 9:00–5:00.
Closed Monday.

Admission: ¥200,
¥100 for high school students.

Asakusa Historical Museum

Ginza Line to Asakusa. Ten-minute walk. See Map 2.

The Asakusa Historical Museum is located on the second and third floors of a nondescript building near the famous Sensoji Temple. A pleasant noodle restaurant anchors the first floor. Few foreigners visit this place, and you will cause a bit of a stir. Most of the exhibits involve cute displays of cardboard characters dancing across backlit display boxes, reminiscent of the shoe-box panorama displays you may have made in primary school. These panoramas are highly technical and artistic.

The second floor is a replica of an old Asakusa street. It is interesting, but nothing special. The third floor has seven mechanical panoramic displays that last three to four minutes. Just push the button and sit down for the show. The displays range from the early days of Asakusa, a courtier's quarter, through the days of the Great Kanto Earthquake of 1923, to the present. The last display is a "Review of Asakusa," where the cardboard characters do a Broadway style review complete with a cancan chorus dance-line. The show ends with a fiery pitch for the old neighborhood, "Ginza, Roppongi, and Shinjuku will never surpass Asakusa!" cries the little cardboard man.

Asakusa Nigiwai Hakubutsukan
2-7-3 Asakusa, Taito-ku, Tokyo
Tel: 3844-5656

Hours: 10:00–7:00.

Admission: ¥700,
¥400 for primary school students,
¥500 for middle school students.

Bunkyo Historical Museum

*Marunouchi Line to Hongo-Sanchome Station. Five-minute walk.
See Map 2.*

The only new thing in this museum is the ultramodern steel-gray architecture that houses the collection. Collectors of phone cards and the like will appreciate this museum's ticket: a plastic card featuring a photograph of the latest special exhibit.

On the first floor there are many artifacts which date back as early as 1690, including pottery, tools, and even an old skeleton. Old photographs, maps, and woodblock prints represent what Bunkyo Ward looked like in the Meiji and Showa eras.

On the second floor, a large tabletop replica of old Bunkyo Ward depicts, both visually and audibly, how this humble ward looked before prefab stucco homes, *pachinko* parlors, and *karaoke* bars. There is a wonderful collection of old *tansu,* ceramics, cookware, shoes, and Noh masks which would make an antique collector envious. Cross over the old-fashioned bridge to the other exhibition room to see a holographic display with believable characters telling you about Bunkyo Ward. Ogai Mori, the ward's famous author, is also idolized. Don't miss the beautiful art-deco stairway.

Bunkyo Furusato Rekishikan
4-9-29 Hongo, Bunkyo-ku, Tokyo
Tel: 3818-7221

Hours: 10:00–5:00.
Closed Monday and 4th Tuesday.

Admission: ¥100,
Children free.

137

Itabashi Historical Museum

Mita Line to Nishi-Takashimadaira Station. Seven-minute walk.

Many of Tokyo's wards have historical museums devoted to the study of what the old neighborhood looked like when it was really old. Most of these efforts are good; this one is excellent. For denizens of central Tokyo, this museum is a long trip, but worth it. The museum fronts on a park, with an artificial lagoon and fountain in the middle. Old men while away their time fishing in the lagoon. The other side of the park is the venue for the Itabashi Art Museum, a dud of a museum.

The Itabashi Historical Museum spans two floors, with audio-visual displays of flora and fauna taking up most of the first floor. Old costumes, maps, and memorabilia are on the second floor. You can blow through the second floor in five minutes, but the displays are tasteful enough to command a bit more time.

By all means, allow five minutes to go out the back door and view the old wooden house. This old wooden structure is full of authentic mockups of rooms in medieval Itabashi Ward. We visited many buildings like this, but still got a kick out of this one.

Itabashi Shiryokan
5-35-25 Akatsuka, Itabashi-ku, Tokyo
Tel: 5998-0081

Hours: 9:00–4:00.
Closed Monday.

Admission: ¥100,
¥50 for children.

Kanagawa Prefecture Museum

Keihin Tohoku Line to Kannai Station. Ten-minute walk.

If you are looking for a microcosm of Kanagawa Prefecture, this is the place. The museum features old Edo-era antiques made of wood and porcelain, a life-size temple which even smells old, geological samples of the earth below, and stuffed models of the flora and fauna of the greater Yokohama area. There is a gorgeous collection on the second floor, including stone and wooden statues found in the Hakone and Kamakura areas. There is something for everyone in this fascinating museum.

The building is one of the last vestiges of old Yokohama and is conveniently located near the Yokohama History Archives and the Yokohama Customs Museum so you can see all three in an afternoon. But reserve a little extra time for this one. The staff is friendly and proud of the collection. This is a must-see in Yokohama.

Kanagawa Kenritsu Hakubutsukan
5-60 Minami-Naka-dori, Naka-ku, Yokohama
Tel: 045-201-0926

Hours: 9:00–4:30.
Closed Monday.

Admission: ¥200,
¥50 for students.

Kita Ward Museum of Provincial History

Nanboku Line to Oji Kamiya Station, Exit 1. Two-minute walk.

This museum provides a home to a collection of artifacts showing life in bygone days in Kita Ward. Huge apartment blocks have sprouted all around the museum. You have to walk through a passageway underneath one to get there. You can hear the housewives beating their futons and gossiping as you approach the entrance.

A fine collection of antiques occupies most of the main display hall, while a second room is full of pottery dug out of the ground in Kita Ward. A small office is placed in between the two; the office workers can barely contain their excitement about having foreign visitors.

Many wards in Tokyo have a historical museum, and this is one of the more modest efforts in terms of architecture and capital expense. Still, the collection is a good one, and the humble surroundings seem suited to the old-fashioned things that adorn the walls.

Kita Kuritsu Kyodo Shiryokan
5-2-12 Oji, Kita-ku, Tokyo
Tel: 3914-4820

Hours: 9:00–5:00.
Closed Monday.   Admission: Free.

Minato Ward Local History Museum

Yamanote, Keihin Tohoku, or Mita Line to Tamachi Station. Two-minute walk. See Map 3.

Minato Ward is one of the most affluent wards in Tokyo, but you wouldn't know it from this mediocre museum. Other wards in Tokyo seem bent on having the newest, most impressive ward museums. Minato marches to the beat of a different drum.

The Minato Ward Museum is located in the ward library, and has all the usual displays, including the obligatory baskets and tools from a bygone era. A replica of an old Japanese house has been placed inside a glass case, and a map of medieval Minato occupies the far wall. The collection is decent, but it takes a lot to impress a visitor after having visited fifteen or twenty ward museums.

The museum is close to the Industrial Safety Museum and the Tamachi campus of Keio University. These are better places to spend your time in Tokyo.

Minato Kuritsu Kyodo Shiryokan
5-28-4 Shiba, Minato-ku, Tokyo
Tel: 3452-4966

Hours: 9:00–5:00.
Closed Sunday.

Admission: Free.

141

Nakano Ward Historical Museum

Seibu Shinjuku Line to Numabukuro Station. Eight-minute walk. Or bus #41 from Nakano Station to Egota-Nichome. Two-minute walk.

This is one of the best historical museums in Tokyo, which is no mean achievement, given the competition. The collection traces the history of Nakano Ward's human settlement from prehistoric times to the present. The permanent collection features ancient pottery, a replica of a seventeenth-century farm community, and a 1930s house and kitchen.

An exhibit area on the second floor is rotated three times a year to feature displays for the New Year, Imari porcelain, and the *Hina Matsuri. Hina Matsuri* is a festival dedicated to little girls, and is commemorated with displays of traditional royal court dolls. The display at the Nakano Museum is the best in Tokyo.

The Nakano Museum has many nice touches, such as traditional Japanese music playing softly in the background, and a reading room with a vista of the garden outside the museum. The staff seems particularly happy to have foreigners visit; a refreshing change from the indifference experienced at similar museums elsewhere in Tokyo.

Yamazaki Kinen Nakano-ku Rekishi Shiryokan
4-3-4 Egota, Nakano-ku, Tokyo
Tel: 3319-9221

Hours: 9:00–5:00.
Closed Monday and the 3rd Sunday
of each month.   Admission: Free.

Ota Ward Folk Museum

Bus from JR Omori Station. Two-minute walk.

Did you know that Ota Ward in Tokyo was a major producer of edible seaweed for Tokyo? Visit the Ota Ward Folk Museum and you will learn this and a host of other valuable facts. You will also spend another pleasant afternoon learning about Japan's history and the evolution of the Tokyo Metropolitan area.

The first floor has little to offer. The second floor displays black-and-white photographs of limited interest. The third floor has exhibits worth waiting for. The obligatory farm instruments and thatched roofs are in evidence, but the life-size costumes and dolls are usually not displayed in ward folk museums. One room is devoted to the science of producing laver, the tasty seaweed that makes the Japanese heart skip a beat.

This museum is very close to the Kumagai Museum, giving you a chance to see a traditional Japanese house and a large folk museum in the same afternoon.

Ota Kuritsu Kyodo Hakubutsukan
5-11-13 Minami-Magome, Ota-ku, Tokyo
Tel: 3777-1070

Hours: 9:00–4:30.
Closed Monday.

Admission: Free.

143

Shinjuku Historical Museum

Marunouchi Line to Yotsuya-Sanchome Station, Exit 4. Seven-minute walk.

Just when you think you can't take another historical museum, you should visit this one—it's a knockout. This place can charm the wings off a butterfly, and should not be missed if you spend any amount of time in Shinjuku (and who doesn't?).

The museum is housed in a modern, steel and glass affair, smack against a steep Japanese garden. The permanent exhibit is in the basement, with sunlight exposure due to the slope of the building. Each exhibit is interesting. You will find a huge model of medieval Shinjuku, examples of old housing, and a replica of an old streetcar station in the middle of the museum showroom.

Luminaries who lived in Shinjuku, including Lafcadio Hearn and favorite-son Soseki Natsume, occupy a special exhibit. Push the buttons and learn about life in Shinjuku in earlier times.

Shinjuku Rekishi Hakubutsukan
22 Saneicho, Shinjuku-ku, Tokyo
Tel: 3359-2131

Hours: 9:00–5:00.
Closed Monday.

Admission: ¥200.

Suginami Ward Historical Museum

Marunouchi Line to Honancho Station. Twenty-minute walk.
Inokashira Line to Eifuku Station. Fifteen-minute walk.

This sparkling new museum is hard to find even by Tokyo standards. Suginami Ward, in a bid to keep up with other wards who were building historical museums at a breakneck pace, completed the museum in May of 1989. It is a pleasant enough place, but you may want to give it a pass unless you live nearby or have an insatiable appetite for history or modern architecture. Building buffs will love the building, but the historical museums of Shinjuku and Bunkyo wards sport better collections.

The first floor has the obligatory displays concerning the geological history of the ward, as well as artifacts such as tools and clothing used by early settlers. One of the video terminals has particularly good videos, buttressed by booming speakers.

The second floor has a small library, meeting rooms, and a terrace. It affords good views of the old farmhouse in the back. The contrast between the farmhouse, lovingly maintained on museum grounds, and the modern museum building, will be one of the most enduring memories of your visit.

Suginami Kuritsu Kyodo Hakubutsukan
1-20-8 Omiya, Suginami-ku, Tokyo
Tel: 3317-0841

Hours: 9:00–5:00.
Closed Monday and the 14th day of
every month.

Admission: ¥100,
¥50 for primary and middle school
students.

Toshima Ward Historical Museum

*Yamanote Line or other train to Ikebukuro Station, West Exit.
Six-minute walk.*

Located in a modern building owned by the Toshima Ward government, the museum contains maps, old wooden tools, and small artifacts collected over the years. The most interesting displays are the mockups of street scenes in old Toshima Ward. The place lacks the luster typical of the best ward museums, but if you live in the area it is worth a visit.

The only feature which distinguishes this museum is the unusually good bulletin board. Many Tokyo museums feature posters of exhibits at other museums, but this might be the champion. A Japanese visitor watched us attempting to decipher the characters; a longtime resident of Toshima Ward, he had turned up to see where all his taxpayer's money was going.

Toshima Kuritsu Kyodo Shiryokan
2-37-4 Nishi-Ikebukuro, Toshima-ku, Tokyo
Tel: 3980-2351

Hours: 9:00–4:30.
Closed Monday and 3rd Sunday.   Admission: Free.

146

Tsukiji Ward Historical Museum

Toei Asakusa Line to Higashi-Ginza Station. Four-minute walk.
See Map 1.

This is a medium-sized, medium-quality historical museum that attracts few visitors. It is located on the first floor of a typical nondescript office building, with scriveners and other civil servants manning the gray desks in an adjacent room. These folks soon got over the shock of having a foreign visitor and were very pleasant.

The best exhibits in the museum depict the growth of the waterfront area of Tokyo. Several exhibits have push-button displays that give explanations in easy Japanese. The rest of the memorabilia are less interesting.

This museum is located near the Kabuki-za, the most famous of Tokyo's Kabuki theaters, but is not in the same vicinity as Tokyo's famous Tsukiji Fish Market. The latter would make an interesting excursion on another occasion.

Tsukiji Kyoiku Kaikan no Kyodo Shiryokan
4-15-1 Tsukiji, Chuo-ku, Tokyo
Tel: 3542-4801

Hours: 9:30–4:30.
Closed Monday. Open 3rd Sunday.   Admission: Free.

Yonbancho Folk Museum

Shinjuku Line to Ichigaya Station, Exit A3. Four-minute walk.
See Map 1.

You really have to love museums or have a particular interest in memorabilia from old Chiyoda Ward to seek out this museum. The little collection occupies a quiet corner in front of a neighborhood public library. Few people know or care about the place.

A visit would be more worthwhile if the collection was more extensive. The few exhibits are interesting: old calculators, old shop signs, and older bric-a-brac are displayed in a few glass cases. It is interesting to compare the sketches and photos of the old neighborhood after picking your way through the skyscrapers to get here.

The collection must be worth something, because a television camera monitors the activities of visitors. Five minutes should be enough of a workout for the camera. If you have more time to kill, browse in the library, reading pop magazines that provide the latest gossip about singers and sumo stars.

Chiyoda Kuritsu Yonbancho Rekishi Minzoku Shiryokan
1 Yonbancho, Chiyoda-ku, Tokyo
Tel: 3238-1139

Hours: 10:00–7:00.
Saturday, 10:00–5:00.
Closed Monday.   Admission: Free.

148

LITERATURE

文学

Hanawa Culture Museum

*Bus #3 from Shibuya Station to Kokugakuin Daigakumae.
One-minute walk. See Map 4.*

Hanawa Hoki-ichi was a scholar who specialized in many things, including the collection of woodblocks used in old Edo (Tokyo) to print Shinto religious material. The museum housing his collection is close to the other museums on the campus of Kokugakuin University.

The museum building is an odd, cellblock-like building with old-fashioned windows. There is a statue of Hanawa near the front entrance, gazing into the distance. The old curator was shocked to see foreigners walk in the door, but he recovered his composure quickly, and was glad to show us around. There is a spooky atmosphere in this museum. The musty shelves are packed with mustier woodblocks, some of which got a lot of use before being retired.

Hanawa is an obscure character today. None of the many people passing by the museum knew anything about him; only the curator could read the Chinese characters used to write his name.

Hanawa Hoki-ichi Kinen Bunka Shiryoshitsu
2-9-1 Higashi, Shibuya-ku, Tokyo
Tel: 3400-3226

Hours: 9:00–5:00, Monday–Friday.
9:00–12:00 on 1st, 3rd, and 5th
Saturdays.   Admission: Free.

150

Japan Calligraphy Museum

Tobu Tojo Line to Tokiwadai Station. Three-minute walk.

The Japan Calligraphy Museum reopened in autumn 1991 after an extensive renovation. The new, improved version is a surprisingly modern venue for a traditional Japanese art form. Students or fans of calligraphy must visit, but others can give the museum a pass. Even serious students of the Japanese language will find it difficult to read the stylized verbiage.

A video room and office occupies the first floor. Visitors buy tickets, don slippers, and take the elevator to the fourth floor, winding their way down stairs at their leisure. Famous and upstart artists are featured here. Unfortunately, the beauty and delicacy of calligraphy are lost on the casual foreign visitor.

Before leaving, we watched the video on the first floor, which showed a state meeting between the emperor and representatives of Bulgaria. What this had to do with calligraphy was lost on us, but the older audience stayed until the end, smiling at their beloved emperor.

Nihon Shodo Bijutsukan
1-3-1 Tokiwa-dai, Itabashi-ku, Tokyo
Tel: 3965-2611

Hours: 10:30–4:00.
Closed Monday and Tuesday.

Admission: ¥800,
¥650 for university students,
¥350 for primary and middle school students.

Japan Museum of Modern Literature

Inokashira Line from Shibuya to Komaba Todaimae. Eight-minute walk.

The area around Todaimae Station has a lot to see, so it is easy to overlook the Japan Museum of Modern Literature. The collection of literary items is on the second floor of a nondescript building. A library occupies most of the first floor.

The most impressive thing in the museum is the excerpt from a manuscript by Soseki Natsume. It seems that Soseki wrote the *furigana* (*hiragana* readings in small type next to difficult *kanji*) himself, and did not leave it to his publisher to clean up the mess so the public could read his books.

The manuscripts of other authors, including Nobel Laureate Yasunari Kawabata, are also displayed under glass. There is no mention of Kawabata's brilliant protégé, Yukio Mishima. Mishima seems permanently banned from museums in Japan. Mishima, the homosexual renaissance man who killed himself after forming his own private cadet force, is a bit too hot to handle in contemporary Japan.

Nihon Kindai Bungakukan
4-3-55 Komaba, Meguro-ku, Tokyo
Tel: 3468-4181

Hours: 9:30–4:30.
Closed Sunday.

Admission: ¥300
(visitors under 18 years not admitted).

Kanagawa Museum of Modern Literature

Bus #11 from Sakuragicho Station. Four-minute walk.

This museum is Yokohama's answer to Tokyo's Museum of Modern Literature. Comparisons are inevitable. This museum, like many of Yokohama's museums, is newer and grander than its counterpart in Tokyo. Unfortunately, neither have great collections.

The Kanagawa Museum of Modern Literature has a coffee shop with fine views of the skyline and bay. Maybe you should spend your time here, because the display rooms are gloomy. The museum displays original manuscripts from illustrious authors such as Soseki Natsume. Like the Japan Museum of Modern Literature, this museum also snubs Japan's most notorious author, Yukio Mishima.

The museum is located in the Yamate area of Yokohama. If you are bored with this museum, it won't take you long to walk to another one that is more to your liking.

Kanagawa Kindai Hakubutsukan
110 Yamatecho, Naka-ku, Yokohama
Tel: 045-622-6666

Hours: 9:30–6:30.
Saturday, Sunday 9:30–5:00.
Closed Monday.   Admission: Free.

Tokyo Metropolitan Museum of Modern Japanese Literature

*Inokashira Line from Shibuya to Komaba Todaimae Station.
Ten-minute walk.*

Don't miss this museum. This is the case even if you don't give a hoot about literature. The museum is located in a beautiful park, in one of the most beautiful mansions you will see in Tokyo or anywhere.

The mansion was built in 1929 by the royal Maeda family, and was reputed to be the finest European-style home in Asia. The building is designed in late English Gothic, replete with French tapestries, Italian marble, and English furniture. The building fell into disrepair during World War II, and was occupied by the American General Matthew Ridgeway during the Allied Occupation.

In 1964, the Tokyo Metropolitan Government took over the building, and a massive renovation returned it to its original splendor. The grounds are spacious and make a lovely setting for a picnic.

The collection is devoted to first editions, handwritten manuscripts, and memorabilia of Japan's most famous writers. Virtually everything is in Japanese. You will not find any photos of the great Yukio Mishima.

Tokyo-to Kindai Bungaku Hakubutsukan
4-3-55 Komaba, Meguro-ku, Tokyo
Tel: 3466-5150

Hours: 9:00–4:30.
Closed 1st and 3rd Mondays and the
day following national holidays.   Admission: Free.

154

Basho Museum

Toei Shinjuku Line to Morishita Station, Exit A1. Seven-minute walk.

The Basho Museum memorializes the life of Matsuo Basho, the poet who lived in seventeenth-century Japan. Basho is remembered for his haiku, and for his extensive travels around Japan. His walk around the entire northern part of Honshu and the poems recording it are feats studied by every Japanese student.

Haiku has its share of foreign adherents, but few know about the Basho Museum. Japanese haiku fans gather in the special tatami room on the second floor to draft and recite the epigrammatic poems. Personal artifacts, haiku, and maps of Basho's travels occupy the second and third floors of the museum.

The museum is surrounded by the nearly obligatory Japanese garden. Winding stone stairs afford you a view of the Sumida River. The nearby Fukagawa Edo Museum is more interesting than the Basho Museum. If you don't have much time, go to the Edo Museum; if you have time or like haiku, visit both.

Basho Kinenkan
1-6-3 Tokiwa, Koto-ku, Tokyo
Tel: 3631-1448

Hours: 10:00–5:00.
Closed Monday.   Admission: ¥100.

155

Goethe Memorial Museum

Nanboku Line to Nishigahara Station, Exit 2. Four-minute walk.

The museum devoted to the life of the great German has given up its forlorn digs in Shibuya and moved to a shiny new home in northern Tokyo. The impressive building is located on Goethe Street, in front of tiny Goethe Park. Tadashi Kogawa, *miso* brewer extraordinaire, founded the museum, contributing his collection of Goethe materials to the permanent collection.

The display room is small, and can be seen in a few minutes. Original German editions of the collected works of Goethe sit by the original editions of Japanese translations of the master's works. One wall is given over to Goethe's family tree. A statue of Goethe rounds out the collection.

The Goethe Museum is not to be confused with the Goethe Institute in Azabu, a lively center of activity for Tokyo's foreign community. If the Goethe Museum seems too trifling to warrant a visit, remember that the Earthquake Science Museum and the Shibusawa Memorial Museum are close by, giving you more than enough to occupy an afternoon of strolling in a quiet corner of blue-collar Tokyo.

Gete Kinenkan
2-30-1 Nishigahara, Kita-ku, Tokyo
Tel: 3918-0828

Hours: 11:00–6:00.
Closed Sunday and Monday.   Admission: Free.

Hayashi Memorial Hall

Seibu Shinjuku Line to Nakai Station. Four-minute walk.

Life was not easy for Fumiko Hayashi, an avant-garde author. Born in Fukuoka Prefecture in 1903, she lived a vagabond existence, moving house often. She began publishing her poetry and married an artist, Ryokubin Tezuka, in 1926. Her most famous works, *Ukigumo* and *Hōrōki,* were written in the house which is now the museum. Her famous writings are proletarian and a bit morose.

Her pride and joy was this house. She and her husband bought the plot of land in 1939 and, after studying almost two-hundred books on architecture and selecting a first-rate carpenter, the building began. Hayashi spent more money and used more space for her kitchen and bathrooms—a novel idea at the time. There are front and back gardens which are especially beautiful in the spring.

The house is huge and consists of many rooms which have been beautifully restored with a fresh coat of paint, wax, and new paper doors. The furniture is sparse, which allows the visitor to appreciate the architecture. The museum opened in April 1992, so the crowds have not yet come to have a look. But with the cheap admission price, friendly staff, and beautiful atmosphere, this won't remain a secret for long.

Hayashi Fumiko Kinenkan
2-20-1 Nakai, Shinjuku-ku, Tokyo
Tel: 5996-9207

Hours: 10:00–4:30.
Closed Monday.

Admission: ¥100,
¥50 for primary and middle school students.

157

Higuchi Memorial Hall

Hibiya Line to Minowa Station. Fifteen-minute walk. See Map 2.

This museum commemorates the life of Ichiyo Higuchi, the most celebrated Japanese female writer of the Meiji era. Higuchi was a novelist, poet, and public figure rolled into one. She lived in *shitamachi* (low city), the traditional, comparatively poor district of northern Tokyo. *Shitamachi* people tend to be fiercely proud, and consider their area a repository of old Japanese culture.

The memorial is located in one of Tokyo's few run-down areas. Not many foreigners visit these parts, so anticipate more stares than usual as you navigate your way to the hard-to-find museum. These streets remind you of what Tokyo must have looked like before it became the world's money machine.

The first floor has a poetry-reading room with excellent woodblock prints on the walls. You can't miss them if you visit the bathroom. The second floor is a weird, atmospheric composite of photos, original manuscripts, and memorabilia. Higuchi's stern eyes follow you as you browse around the room. Everything in her life seems to be covered; from her early writings to the commemorative stamp in 1981.

Higuchi Ichiyo Kinenkan
3-18-4 Ryusen, Taito-ku, Tokyo
Tel: 3873-0004

Hours: 9:00–4:00.
Closed Monday.

Admission: ¥100,
¥50 for children.

Iwasaki Art Museum

Seibu Shinjuku Line to Kami-Igusa Station. Ten-minute walk.

Chihiro Iwasaki was one of Japan's most beloved writers of children's books. This bright, modern museum is connected to her restored atelier, and provides a home for a collection of her books. The layout of the museum allows little boys the excitement of running up and down stairs to explore the warren-like fastness of the museum. The unusual architecture is more interesting than the watercolor illustrations for her books. A teahouse occupies the top floor, providing nice views of the surrounding neighborhood and a chance to rest your feet.

The first-floor video room airs a documentary about the tragic Hiroshima and Nagasaki bombings. This may seem irrelevant to a museum devoted to children's books. Japan's preoccupation with the atomic bombings, with daily references on television or in national newspapers, can get on the nerves of American residents. However, Iwasaki seemed genuinely pacific, without a political agenda to sell to the population. In this light, the antiwar literature that adorns the museum has a powerful appeal.

Iwasaki Chihiro Ehon Bijutsukan
4-7-2 Shimo-Shakujii, Nerima-ku, Tokyo
Tel: 3995-0612

Hours: 10:00–5:00.
Closed Monday.
Open until 7:00 on Fridays.

Admission: ¥500,
¥200 for middle and
high school students,
¥100 for primary school students.

Kumagai Memorial Hall

Oimachi Line to Ebaramachi Station. Bus to Manpukuji.

Skip the Japan Calligraphy Museum and go here instead. Tsuneko Kumagai was one of Japan's most distinguished calligraphers and her house has been converted to a museum memorializing her life and work. Other museums of this type have grander houses and gardens, but the Kumagai Museum has been restored and is a peaceful place to spend some leisure time.

Kumagai was born in Kyoto in 1894, but moved to Tokyo for the bright lights and the big city. She married at age twenty-one, but didn't let the drudgery of the Japanese housewife interfere with her art. She practiced calligraphy her entire life, leaving some of the best examples in this museum. The second floor has a nice, bright library, packed with books and brushes. The adjacent room gives you the chance to pull up a cushion and practice calligraphy. One page per customer, please.

The first floor has a collection of photos of Kumagai, including a family treasure: a picture of the master with the emperor's wife.

If you make your way out here, don't miss a chance to see the Ota Ward Folk Museum, only five minutes away by foot.

Kumagai Tsuneko Kinenkan
4-5-15 Minami-Magome, Ota-ku, Tokyo
Tel: 3773-0123

Hours: 9:00–4:30.
Closed Monday.   Admission: ¥100.

Osaragi Memorial Museum

Bus #11 from Sakuragicho Station. Four-minute walk.

Jiro Osaragi was the James Michener of Japan. He was one of the most famous of a school of writers specializing in historical novels. Numerous plays and movies are based on his works. He was also one of the few Japanese authors to attract international attention in the post World War II era.

Osaragi was a *Hamakko*—a native of Yokohama. The Yokohama city government has opened a magnificent museum commemorating the life of its favorite son. Photos and heirlooms adorn the first floor; a collection of his novels is on the second floor. An entire room is devoted to Osaragi's collection of books, maps, and pictures of Paris.

Osaragi loved cats almost as much as he loved France and his beloved Yokohama. Little statues of the beasts can be found everywhere. The museum contains a particularly charming series of old photos showing Osaragi playing with a snow white cat.

Osaragi Jiro Kinenkan
113 Yamatecho, Naka-ku, Yokohama
Tel: 045-622-5002

Hours: 10:00–5:00.
Closed Monday.

Admission: ¥200,
¥100 for primary and middle school students.

Sato Memorial Museum

Chiyoda Line to Nezu Station. Five-minute walk. See Map 2.

Hachiro Sato was the Dr. Seuss of Japan. A generation of Japanese was raised on his children's books and songs. The hard-bitten writer was born in Tokyo but was a big fan of Nagoya's Chunichi Dragons baseball team. Nearly every photo in the display shows him in a Dragons jacket, puffing a cigarette.

If you are looking for an unusual museum, this is likely to please you. It is more like visiting someone's home than visiting a museum. The relics and memorabilia are crammed into a little room, complete with the composer's piano and Sony tape recorder, which croons out Sato's hits such as "Red Apple." Sing along if you like.

The staff seems genuinely happy to have foreign visitors and will treat you well. For the many Japanese who pack the place, it is a nostalgic experience. Copies of Sato's books can be read while sitting on the comfortable sofa next to the garden. Sato's widow lives upstairs, and answers the phone when you call to verify hours. Don't call too early, she likes to sleep late.

Sato Hachiro Kinenkan
2-16-1 Yayoi, Bunkyo-ku, Tokyo
Tel: 3812-3080

Hours: 1:00–5:00.
Only open on Tuesday and
Saturday.   Admission: Free.

MUSIC

音楽

Drum Museum

Ginza Line to Tawaramachi Station. Also an easy walk from Asakusa Station. See Map 2.

Few museums in Tokyo are as delightful as the Drum Museum. Located on the second floor of an old family store specializing in the sale of musical instruments and Buddhist shrines, the museum has some of the best tribal art in all of Japan. Drums from more than forty countries, bilingual explanations, and a particularly good set of audio-visual displays make this museum a must-see.

Admission to the museum is paid at a counter in the middle of the busy store. You then enter a large soundproof room crammed with fascinating examples of drums from around the world. You can view drums disguised as pieces of furniture from Burkina Fasso, Tibetan drums made from skulls, and Nepalese tambourines.

Children, and adults who have never quite grown up, will enjoy testing the acoustical ability of the collection. The exhibits are color coded to indicate drummability. Red means off limits, blue means bang the drum softly. Many of the kids who visit ignore the blues and bang away. Particularly noisome are the English bass drums which emit sounds fit for a Mahler symphony. The more delicate Moroccan models sit mournfully opposite; look, but don't touch.

Taiko-kan
2-1-1 Nishi-Asakusa, Taito-ku, Tokyo
Tel: 3842-5622

Hours: 10:00–5:00.
Closed Monday and Tuesday.

Admission: ¥300,
¥150 for children.

Koga Memorial Museum

Odakyu Line or Chiyoda Line to Yoyogi Uehara. Three-minute walk from the station.

Masao Koga was the Irving Berlin of Japan. He was the first Japanese musician to combine traditional Japanese melodies with Western tonal scales. The combination gave birth to *enka*—the ubiquitous pop music sung in *karaoke* bars throughout Japan.

Koga was nothing for looks, and *enka* is, at best, an acquired taste, but a visit to this museum is highly recommended.

Koga was born in Japan, but spent his youth in Japanese-occupied Korea. He was deeply impressed by the exotic music of Korea. Michio Miyagi, the *koto* artist whose house has also been turned into a splendid museum in Iidabashi, also spent his youth in Korea and adopted the indigenous music in his own compositions.

The Koga Museum is surrounded by pretty gardens. Don't visit the museum without at least a few minutes to wander in the seclusion of the gardens.

Koga Masao Kinen Hakubutsukan
3-6-12 Uehara, Shibuya-ku, Tokyo
Tel: 3460-9051

(A new museum building is presently being constructed and will be opened to the public in September 1994.)

165

Miyagi Memorial Hall

Sobu Line to Iidabashi Station, West Exit. Yurakucho and Tozai subway lines to Iidabashi. Ten-minute walk.

Anyone interested in Japanese music or traditional Japanese culture should visit this museum. It is one of the few small museums in Tokyo that is truly bilingual. The exhibits have English translations and a free English cassette tape telling the life story of Michio Miyagi—one of the greatest Japanese musicians of the twentieth century.

Miyagi became blind when he was seven years old, and began studying the *koto*—an instrument historically played by blind people. Miyagi spent part of his childhood in Korea, and was deeply impressed with the exoticism of Korean music.

The museum has many attractive exhibits, including a videotape of Miyagi playing his most famous work, *Haru no Umi* (The Spring Sea), and interesting displays showing part of his record collection as well as photos showing him performing with famous violinists.

This museum is best visited on a nice day because of the garden behind the main building. You can enjoy the ambience and see the spare room where the old Miyagi taught his last students.

Miyagi Michio Kinenkan
35 Naka-machi, Shinjuku-ku, Tokyo
Tel: 3269-0208

Hours: 10:00–4:00.
Closed Monday, Tuesday, 2nd, 4th, and 5th Sundays.

Admission: ¥400,
¥300 for middle school students,
¥200 for primary school students.

Music Box Museum

Yurakucho Line to Gokokuji Station. Five-minute walk.

This odd museum combines staid exhibition viewing with performance art. When you visit the Music Box Museum, you are entitled to hear performances using the extensive collection. Be prepared to hear over and over "Bicycle Built for Two" and other popular hits.

The collection of music boxes spans two floors of a nondescript apartment building. The entrance is on the second floor, where the ¥800 "show" takes place. The proprietors will push you to pay for and view the more extensive ¥1300 show on the third floor. You are asked to make prior reservations but there is always room for more. The collection is good and lends a feeling of nostalgia to a visit. However, a little bit of nostalgia goes a long way, and the ordinarily curious may be fed up with the long show. Be prepared to spend between an hour and an hour and a half on the presentation. If you love music boxes, you will love this place, but other visitors may leave with their ears ringing.

Orugoru no Chisana Hakubutsukan
3-25-14 Mejiro-dai, Bunkyo-ku, Tokyo
Tel: 3941-0008

Hours: Open daily.
Reserve in advance.

Admission: ¥1300 for main show, ¥800 for smaller show which starts 30 minutes after the main show.

167

Musical Instruments Museum

Seibu Ikebukuro Line to Ekoda Station. Five-minute walk.

This museum is one of Tokyo's best kept secrets. It is one of our favorite museums. If you are a musician this is a must, but even if you don't play an instrument you won't be bored. The museum has an awesome collection of instruments from practically every country or region around the world. From Austria to Zaire, there are drums, brass, gongs, bells, winds, pianos, strings—you name it, it's here. The museum even has a full set of instruments for an Indonesian gamelan orchestra.

Each region of the world is divided into ten classrooms which display rare, new, old, exotic, and kitsch instruments. The displays are bilingual and the photographs on the wall display the locals in native costumes playing the instruments.

The curator, a French-horn enthusiast and an avid fan of the Chicago Symphony's Dale Clevenger, is very helpful in explaining the collection. The area around the music academy is lively with music students waiting to make their mark on the music scene. Even the streets have classical music playing on the loudspeaker system.

Musashino Ongaku Daigaku Gakki Hakubutsukan
1-13 Hazawa, Nerima-ku, Tokyo
Tel: 3992-1121, Ext. 243

Hours: 10:00–3:00, Wednesdays
only.
Appointment necessary other times.   Admission: Free.

Sogakudo Museum

JR Yamanote Line to Ueno Station, Ueno Koen Exit. Four-minute walk. See Map 2.

Japan has embraced Western classical music with a vengeance. In some Tokyo neighborhoods, classical music discs constitute twenty percent of the sales. Only Austria can confidently boast of citizenry more well versed in Beethoven than the Japanese.

It all started here. The Sogakudo school was the first classical-music conservatory in Japan worthy of the name. In typical Japanese fashion, a handful of Western experts were imported for short periods of technology transfer. The Japanese have never looked back, and now operate a huge industry devoted to the study and performance of Western music.

The Sogakudo school was renovated in the late 1980s. The new paint job and restoration have done wonders for its demeanor. The display rooms have photos of the Japanese and Western founders of the school, but the best thing to see is the organ on the top floor, the first of its kind in Japan. Suntory Hall may boast a more modern organ, but if Saint-Saens woke up tomorrow, he would want his organ symphony performed here.

Sogakudo
8-43 Ueno Koen, Taito-ku, Tokyo
Tel: 3824-1988

Hours: 9:30–4:30
Sunday, Tuesday, and Thursday.

Admission: ¥200,
¥100 for children, primary and
middle school students.

169

Suntory Museum

Ginza or Marunouchi Line to Akasaka Mitsuke Station.
Three-minute walk. See Map 1.

The ubiquitous Suntory Corporation has a museum worthy of its high-powered cultural image. The museum is located on the tenth floor of a building looming over Akasaka. The view is great. Sometimes, the traveling collection is too.

Suntory Corporation built one of the finest concert halls in the world just down the road from this museum, and the exhibitions usually focus on musicians or artists. The Mahler, Chopin, and Tchaikovsky exhibitions were particularly memorable. Unfortunately, the more avant-garde composers are never going to get much exposure here, or anywhere else in Japan.

The museum usually has an excellent video playing, and sometimes has a string quartet or soloist performing as well, thus justifying the relatively high ticket price. If you can afford an extended visit, go around 2:00 or 3:00 in the afternoon, popular times for the concert performances.

Santori Bijutsukan
1-2-3 Moto-Akasaka, Minato-ku, Tokyo
Tel: 3470-1073

Hours: 10:00–5:00.
10:00–7:00 on Friday.
Closed Monday.

Admission: ¥1000,
¥700 for students.

NATURAL SCIENCE

自然科学

Insect Wander World

*Seibu Ikebukuro Line from Ikebukuro to Toshimaen Station.
Three-minute walk.*

If crowded Tokyo is starting to bug you, go look at its bugs. This pleasant little museum is nestled in the back of an amusement park; admission can be free since you must purchase a ticket to enter the park to get to the Insectarium. The book of coupons included in the stiff ¥3000 admission price allows you to ride on ferris wheels or other rides, or to look at the bugs for only one coupon.

The Insectarium can be seen in five minutes; bug fiends can linger for more than an hour. The display depicts insect life in Japan, with charts, photos, and live examples in glass cases. A butterfly exhibit is housed outdoors in a messy hothouse. A visit will not give you the creeps.

Several footpaths link the remote Insectarium with ground zero of the amusement park. One of them is woodsy and quiet, a nice break from the teeny-bopper madness near the roller-coasters.

Toshimaen Konchukan
3-25-1 Koyama, Nerima-ku, Tokyo
Tel: 3990-3131

Admission: ¥100,
or one amusement park coupon.
(Park admission fee: ¥3000.)

Hours: 10:00–5:00.

Nature Study Park and Museum

Yamanote Line to Meguro Station, East Exit. Ten-minute walk.
See Map 3.

When you get to the point where you can't stand the crowding and chaos of Tokyo, head for this museum. This is actually a small exhibit hall in the middle of a large nature preserve administered by the Institute for Nature Study. It is one of the few places in metropolitan Tokyo where you feel like you are in the wilderness. The area is crisscrossed by trails leading you through forest and swampland. In many places, the only sound is bird song.

This museum in central Tokyo has its origins six hundred years ago, when the Shirokane clan built a house on the present grounds. Later, owners developed the grounds into an imperial estate. In 1949, the grounds came under the jurisdiction of the Institute for Nature Study.

The small fieldhouse may be an anticlimax after the relative solitude of this walk but the ambitious visitor will be rewarded with information about the geological history of Tokyo, and displays showing samples of "unique" Japanese soil.

You should combine a visit to this urban wilderness with the nearby Tokyo Teien Art Museum, an art-deco wonder five minutes from the front gate.

Shizen Kyoikuen
5-21-5 Shirokane-dai, Minato-ku, Tokyo
Tel: 3441-7176

Hours: 9:00–4:00 (5:00 in summer).
Closed Monday.

Admission: ¥200,
¥60 for middle and
high school students.

173

Parasitological Museum

Yamanote Line to Meguro Station, West Exit. Fifteen-minute walk or take the bus to Otori Jinjamae (2 stops).

The Meguro Parasitological Museum is the only one of its kind in the world. The museum occupies the two floors of a medical laboratory devoted to the study of parasites and parasitological diseases. Anyone with an interest in medicine will enjoy a visit. The whole museum can be seen in ten minutes, but the curious can spend much longer.

Some visitors might think that this museum is a bit ghoulish, but the displays are informative. Anyone planning to travel to a third-world country should visit the museum because they are sure to come away with a better understanding of tropical diseases and how to avoid them.

The museum has displays of common diseases caused by parasites, with graphic photos of the victims. Especially interesting are the maps depicting areas infected by the major types of parasites. A large map of Japan is electronically wired to show infected areas.

Actual samples of parasites are displayed in clear vials, and a three-meter-long tapeworm occupies part of one wall. Most displays have brief English translations, but the photos and diagrams help lessen the the language barrier.

Kiseichukan
4-1-1 Shimo, Meguro-ku, Tokyo
Tel: 3716-1264

Hours: 10:00–5:00.
Closed Monday and national
holidays.   Admission: Free.

174

Sunshine International Aquarium

Yamanote Line or other train to Ikebukuro Station, exit for Sunshine City. Five-minute walk.

The Sunshine International Aquarium is located on the top floor of a huge ten-story building next door to the even larger Sunshine City, the tallest building in northern Tokyo. The aquarium is the world's highest, and is home to 20,000 fish from around the world. The most interesting denizen is a huge oarfish, whose appearance on local beaches is said to presage big earthquakes. Take advantage of a discount ticket which enables you to see the planetarium, aquarium, and Ancient Orient Museum, all in Sunshine City, for a bargain price.

The Japanese have created an aquarium with a theatrical flair. The long lines to get in are made more tolerable by the trained seals performing on a stage near the ticket booth. The seals seem to be able to understand Japanese, putting them in the first ranks of the Tokyo expat community in this regard.

The aquarium has lifelike displays—especially the Amazon jungle tank. The fish seem to be happier here than on a sushi plate.

Sanshain Kokusai Suizokukan
World Import Mart 10th Floor,
3-1-3 Higashi-Ikebukuro, Toshima-ku, Tokyo
Tel: 3989-3466

Hours: 10:00–6:00.
10:00–6:30 on Sundays.

Admission: ¥1440,
¥720 for children.

175

Tokyo Bird Park

Monorail from Hamamatsucho Station to Ryutsu Sentamae Station. Fifteen-minute walk.

Tokyo is a city that never ceases to surprise you. Who would ever expect to find a fairly decent birdwatching glen within the concrete and smog of the city limits? Tokyo has it, within the vast expanse of the harbor, providing the necessary seclusion to keep the birds from heading to Hakone. The grounds are spacious with several ponds, hills, and natural gardens. What a great place to have a picnic!

The birds can be viewed from an outdoor blind or an indoor rotunda. The outdoor blind includes good telescopes free of charge. The indoor rotunda has floor-to-ceiling windows as well as telescopes. The truly lazy can sit on plush couches while watching the aviatic comings and goings of the birds on overhead color monitors, with Bose speakers broadcasting the chirping.

The Bird Park can be visited along with the regular Heiwajima Antique Fair. Information about the fair can be had by calling 3980-8228. This fair is a great place to browse and compare prices if you are interested in Japanese antiques. Even if you couldn't care less about birds or antiques, you won't be bored by the monorail train ride zipping along the waterfront.

Tokyo-ko Yacho Koen
Tokyo Harbor, 3-1 Tokai, Ota-ku, Tokyo
Tel: 3799-5031

Hours: 9:00–4:30.

Admission: ¥200,
¥100 for primary school children,
infants free.

Tokyo Metropolitan Takao Museum of Nature Science

Keio Line to Takaosanguchi Station. Five-minute walk.

The Takao Museum has one of the most beautiful settings of any museum in Tokyo, a city more famous for smog than pine trees. The Takao Museum is perched in the foothills of Mount Takao, a popular hiking spot in the mountainous area west of Tokyo. This is a great spot for a day trip if you have forgotten what fresh air smells like.

The museum is located next to the Takao Youth Hostel, and concentrates on the geology, flora, and fauna of the Tokyo area in general, and the Mount Takao area in particular. The first floor displays artist's conceptions of aerial views of Tokyo Harbor at two-thousand-year intervals, vividly displaying how earthquakes have reshaped the local landscape.

The second floor has several interesting slide shows featuring the birds and wildlife that prowl the area. If you have any thoughts of hiking in order to see the critters up close, you should visit the second floor before setting off on the trails. A replica of the entire area gives you a good idea of the best trails and most interesting routes.

Tokyo-to Takao Shizen Kagaku Hakubutsukan
2436 Takao-machi, Hachioji-shi, Tokyo
Tel: 0426-61-0305

Hours: 9:00–4:00.
Closed 1st and 3rd Mondays.   Admission: Free.

Yumenoshima Tropical Plant Dome

Yurakucho Line to Shin-Kiba. Eight-minute walk.

The Tropical Plant Dome is a fine recreation of a rainforest, with hundreds of exotic plants ensconced in a huge atrium. Japanese families mob the place on the weekends, craning their necks to see the strange flowers. If you don't mind the crowds, it is a nice place to spend a cold winter afternoon in Tokyo.

The exhibits surrounding the dome are just as interesting. Particularly interesting is the film shown at a small theater that depicts life in small villages in Cameroon, West Africa. Other exhibits show products made from tropical plants, including an interesting array of pharmaceutical products.

The Tropical Plant Dome is located in one of Tokyo's nicer areas of parkland and provides a rare chance for peace and quiet in this unquiet city. Visitors to the Tropical Plant Dome can also visit the nearby Lucky Dragon Display House and feast at the wonderful, cheap Chinese restaurant in Shin-Kiba Station.

Yumenoshima Nettai Shokubutsukan
3-2 Yumenoshima, Koto-ku, Tokyo
Tel: 3522-0281

Hours: 9:30–4:00.
Closed Monday.

Admission: ¥200, ¥100 for middle and primary school students.

SCIENCE

科学

Earthquake Science Museum

Nanboku Line to Nishigahara Station, Exit 2. Five-minute walk.

Every time Tokyo is shaken by a little tremor, its residents are seized by a moment of terror. One of these days, the tremor will not stop after a few seconds, but will grow to frightening levels. Almost everyone in this town is afraid of the Big One, and the displays at the Earthquake Science Museum do nothing to dispel their fears.

Video displays tell you the grim facts of life about the tremendous damage caused by earthquakes, and the impending doom that Tokyo faces. A superb little earthquake library has all of the latest Japanese language books; printing such books seems to have become a cottage industry in these parts.

The building next door to the museum has rooms with machines that simulate the biggest earthquakes in history. The machines are only turned on when large groups of people visit the museum. Individual visitors must be content with a tour of the fire prevention center on the roof.

You are encouraged to try your skill firing a fire extinguisher at fixed targets. The old man who gives you the tour winces when you ask him "When is the Big One going to hit?" He sighs, and looks at the horizon, "It is already overdue . . . we expect it any day . . ."

Jishin no Kagakukan
Nishigahara 2-chome, Ichiban Rokugo, Kita-ku, Tokyo
Tel: 3940-3494

Hours: 9:00–5:00. Closed Monday.   Admission: Free.

Gotoh Planetarium and Astronomical Museum

Yamanote Line to Shibuya, East Exit. See Map 4.

Located on the eighth floor of the mammoth movie-theater building across from the station, the Gotoh Planetarium is a copy of the best planetariums in the US and Europe. Every detail has been lovingly reproduced. Only the schmaltzy music during the show has been added.

The planetarium shows Tokyo's sky as it appears from atop the Tokyo Dome on a clear, dark night. The show changes regularly, but usually focuses on Japanese legends concerning the stars. The narrative is in fairly easy Japanese to accommodate the many children.

The Astronomical Museum is built in a circle around the showroom. The show begins with replicas of the first European telescopes and includes paintings of astronomical heavies such as Copernicus and Keppler. The most interesting exhibits concern Japanese legends about constellations. Many of the constellations were thought to represent traditional Japanese musical instruments.

Few foreigners visit the planetarium, and you must be prepared for the usual routine of stares and giggles. The Japanese children can go home and tell their friends that there were extraterrestrials in the room during the sky show.

Tenmon Hakubutsukan to Gotoh Puranetariumu
2-21-12 Shibuya, Shibuya-ku, Tokyo
Tel: 3407-7409

Hours: 10:00–6:00.
Closed Monday.
Shows are every 90 minutes.

Admission: ¥700,
¥400 for primary and
middle school students.

Itabashi Science and Education Center

Tobu Tojo Line to Kami-Itabashi. Three-minute walk.

This pretty new museum is crawling with kids pushing display buttons and running amok. However, the museum has an ace in the hole—an earthquake simulation machine in the basement.

You wait your turn and climb aboard, fastening your seat belt before turning on the machine. A television monitor tells you the magnitude of the earthquake on the Japanese scale. The simulation only goes as high as six, making you wonder what a seven must feel like.

Other exhibits in the basement will keep the kiddies occupied for at least thirty minutes. The lights are so bright that you feel sunglasses must be in order. A futuristic soundproofed room showing a video about Itabashi Ward in the year 2000 is a bit of a disappointment; it doesn't look much different than the neighborhood you saw on the way from the train station.

Itabashi Kuritsu Kyoiku Kagakukan
4-14-1 Tokiwa-dai, Itabashi-ku, Tokyo
Tel: 3559-6561

Hours: 9:00–4:30.
Closed 3rd Monday of every month.   Admission: Free.

National Science Museum

Yamanote Line or Ginza Line to Ueno Station. Ten-minute walk.
See Map 2.

Kids will love it, adults will get footsore, but hardly anyone has the stamina to see everything in this vast museum. It is located in Ueno Park, which has people and museums galore.

The main building is a beautiful stone-and-brick affair, with vaulted ceilings and Lalique-style glasswork. The exhibits are interesting but unfortunately the display is poor. It is simply too dark to see well. More exhibits await you in the many annexes. The museum has displays of clocks, earthquakes, glassblowing, aviation, space exploration—you name it, they've got it. Zero fighters, plate tectonics, and Hachiko, the famous dog, are the most popular exhibits. The most popular rooms are packed with rambunctious children. Don't expect a quiet afternoon.

If all of this commotion bothers you, retreat to the interior courtyard and look at the spacecraft. Lifesize models of the latest toys from the Kagoshima Space Center stand like sentinels over the mobs of squealing children.

Kokuritsu Kagaku Hakubutsukan
7-20 Ueno Koen, Koto-ku, Tokyo
Tel: 3822-0111

Hours: 9:00–4:30.
Closed Monday.

Admission: ¥400,
¥70 for children.

183

Oxygen Museum

Mekama Line to Fudomae Station. Four-minute walk.

This is a gas of a museum. The collection of oxygen bottles and machinery is housed in an old building resembling somebody's garage. The doors are open all day so everything is covered with a fine layer of Tokyo grime. Nihon Sanso, the industrial giant that runs the place, could probably afford to do better.

Standing guard in this benighted place, like an icon in a gas station, is a statute of Korekiyo Takahashi. Takahashi was the greatest Japanese politician of the twentieth century. He was not an official of Nihon Sanso, but his friendship with corporate moguls was instrumental in Nihon Sanso's acquisition of advanced gas technology from the US and Europe. Takahashi used his extensive contacts abroad to get technology badly needed in Japan.

We saw few memorials to Takahashi in Tokyo; he seems forgotten by later generations. Now his likeness stands in a forgotten museum that few people know about and fewer visit.

Nihon Sanso Kinenkan
5-25-2 Nishi-Gotanda, Shinagawa-ku, Tokyo
Tel: 3491-3865

Hours: 9:00–5:00.   Admission: Free.

Science Foundation Museum

Tozai Line to Kudanshita or Takebashi Station. Five-minute walk to Kitanomaru Park. See Map 1.

This is yet another science museum in central Tokyo. The museum was founded by the Japan Science and Technology Promotion Foundation, and was opened in 1964. The exhibits sprawl over five floors, and include space development, nuclear energy, steel, and consumer electronics.

The modern displays are a bit of a surprise, after an uninspiring entrance and a slightly seedy cafeteria looming on the right. Children will like the museum, and technological adults may also like it. However, the displays are not as good as the huge National Science Museum in Ueno Park. You should visit this museum only if you are a science buff, or have time to kill while walking in beautiful Kitanomaru Park. The National Museum of Modern Art Crafts Gallery is located in the same park. Why not visit both?

Kagaku Gijutsukan
2-1 Kitanomaru Koen, Chiyoda-ku, Tokyo
Tel: 3212-8471

Hours: 9:30–4:50.

Admission: ¥515, ¥310 for students.

185

Sunshine International Planetarium

*Yamanote Line or other trains to Ikebukuro Station, East Exit.
Ten-minute walk.*

Galileo would have a field day at this place—if he did not have
to wait in the long lines. More high-tech than the Gotoh
Planetarium in Shibuya, the numerous displays are bright
and interesting. The light show is held in a large, modern
auditorium, but a star is a star no matter how you are seated.
The Gotoh Planetarium does however have the edge in the
museum-like display that surrounds the theater.

The place is packed, especially on the weekends and during
the holidays, so trying to do all three museums within this
mega complex may be a bit tough—better drink one of those
salaryman pep drinks for energy!

Sanshain Puranetariumu
3-1-3 Higashi-Ikebukuro, Toshima-ku, Tokyo
Tel: 3989-3475

Hours: 11:00–5:00, Monday–
Friday.
11:00–6:00, Saturday.
10:00–6:00, Sunday.

Admission: ¥800,
¥500 for children up to and
including primary school.

Tepco Electric Energy Museum

Yamanote Line to Shibuya Station. Ten-minute walk. See Map 4.

This glowing museum covers seven floors in the heart of trendy Shibuya. The museum is a virtual temple to Tokyo Electric Power Co., the Commonwealth Edison of Japan. Cute office ladies, clad in perky uniforms and pillbox hats, scamper around speaking breathy *keigo* (polite Japanese). The whole place spins with energy. This museum displays all of the major uses of electrical energy coupled with detailed explanations about the various sources of energy.

A comprehensive description of the exhibits would make this a treatise. Suffice to say that every conceivable use of electricity is represented in this museum, usually in a tasteful and interesting display. Women visitors will be interested in the kitchen of the future, with computer-assisted plumbing and kitchen cabinets with LCD monitors. Males may groove on the nuclear power displays and electronic toys. School-aged children will marvel at the latest computer and electronic toys of all types.

Tokyo is packed with nice museums, but the Energy Museum is particularly worthwhile. Only a philistine would deliberately avoid Shibuya, and hardly anything in this area is cheap, let alone free.

Denryokukan
1-12-10 Jinnan, Shibuya-ku, Tokyo
Tel: 3477-1191

Hours: 10:30–6:30.
Closed Wednesday.   Admission: Free.

187

Waterworks Museum

JR or subway to Shinjuku Station. Six-minute walk from West Exit.
Located next door to the Hilton Hotel in the Shinjuku Kokusai
Building. See Map 5.

This museum is not only free, you get gifts for passing through the entrance. Most visitors are given a bar of soap, a wrench, and water conservation devices to place inside faucets. The displays occupy most of the first floor of the Shinjuku Kokusai Building, in the shadow of Tokyo's gigantic city hall.

The exhibition rooms trace the history of public water supply in the Tokyo area from water bucket days to the present. There are many do-it-yourself displays that kids love. Since many of them were broken during our visit, the visitors must have been a little rough.

This museum will answer some of life's burning questions, such as how much water is used to flush a toilet (eighteen liters), as well as how water is filtered before it reaches your home. The reception area also has an English-language handout, *Waterworks in Tokyo 1986,* to commemorate your visit.

The Waterworks Museum is cheerful, and is a good stop if you are walking around West Shinjuku.

Tokyo-to Suido Kinenkan
6-6-2 Nishi-Shinjuku, Shinjuku-ku, Tokyo
Tel: 3346-0354

Hours: 9:30–4:30.   Admission: Free.

188

SPORT

スポーツ

Baseball Hall of Fame and Museum

JR Sobu Line to Suidobashi West Exit, or Mita Line to Suidobashi. Five-minute walk from either station, exit to Gate 21 of the Tokyo Dome. See Map 2.

The Tokyo Baseball Hall of Fame may not match the original American version in Cooperstown, but it is worth a visit.

The museum is located inside the huge Tokyo Dome, on the site of the old Korakuen Stadium where many of the heroics took place. You enter the museum at street level, and descend into the basement for a series of excellent exhibition rooms. You can see the uniforms and autographed baseballs of luminaries such as Kaneda, Oh, and Kinugasa. The "Three D Theatre" follows, where you don plastic glasses to watch a ten minute tape of a batting clinic by Sadaharu Oh. More interesting are the exhibition halls including Cooperstown-style plaques of the inductees. So far, Viktor Sarkin, the great Russian pitcher, is the only foreign member of the Hall of Fame.

No Japanese museum would be complete without some kind of high-tech touch, and the Hall of Fame has several video stations and a computer database, courtesy of IBM. The museum also has an excellent library, with a musty smell and tranquility reminiscent of the Cooperstown counterpart. The librarian is a bit nervous when foreigners are around.

Yakyu Taiiku Hakubutsukan
1-3-61 Koraku, Bunkyo-ku, Tokyo
Tel: 3811-3600

Hours: 10:00–5:00.
Closed Monday.

Admission: ¥350,
¥150 for children.

Bicycle Culture Center

Ginza Line to Toranomon or Marunouchi Line to Kokkaigijido-mae.
Near Hotel Okura and American Embassy. Ten-minute walk.
See Map 1.

Japan's spectacularly successful export drive began in earnest with massive bicycle exports in the 1930s. Consequently, the collection in this museum is of interest to the general public as well as bicycle enthusiasts.

The exhibition room on the second floor is crammed with old bicycles and memorabilia. The first bicycles made in Japan are displayed opposite antique French posters touting the glories of bike riding. Other early posters resemble wood-block prints, with clunky bikes traveling along beside misty Mount Fuji.

Most exhibits have English translations, and are arranged in an attractive, chronological fashion. The cognoscenti will want to spend hours, but you can see the entire display in fifteen or twenty minutes.

The museum is close to the Okura Museum, Tokyo Tower, the NHK Broadcast Museum, and other cultural buildings such as Suntory Hall.

Jitensha Bunka Senta
Jitensha Kaikan No. 3 Building,
1-9-3 Akasaka, Minato-ku, Tokyo
Tel: 3584-4530

Hours: 10:00–4:00.
Closed Saturday and Wednesday.   Admission: Free.

Equine Museum

JR to Negishi Station. Six-minute walk.

The Equine Museum is Yokohama's answer to Tokyo's Horse Racing Museum, and it is just as spectacular. The Equine Museum is devoted to the history of horses, as beasts of burden and animals that people bet on.

The collection includes numerous statues of horses, old carriages, and an incredible collection of photos. We are not fans of horse racing, but people who are will love the place. It would take two or three hours to see all the displays.

The Equine Museum is not far from the Trolley Car Museum, in what is otherwise an uninteresting part of Yokohama. If you have limited time and no interest in trolley cars or horses, it is better to concentrate on the waterfront area of Yokohama.

Uma no Hakubutsukan
Negishi Racing Memorial Park,
1-3 Negishi-dai, Naka-ku, Yokohama
Tel: 045-662-7581

Hours: 9:30–4:30.
Closed Monday.

Admission: ¥100,
¥30 for primary, middle, and
high school students.

Horse Racing Museum

Keio Line to Higashi-Fuchu Station. Fifteen-minute walk. On racing days, a shuttle train runs from Higashi-Fuchu to Keibajo-mae. Five-minute walk.

If you have spent all your money horsing around at the track you can still visit this museum—it's free. Regulars visit this museum early in the morning before placing bets to get the latest information on their favorite fillies. Leave it to the Japanese to computerize horse racing. You do not have to visit the stud farms or talk to the jockies to get the background of a horse—all the information you need can be easily accessed in several computers. However, you should go early as the lines can be long.

There are many oil paintings and bronze sculptures of Japan's famous horses. These are the horses that did not end up at the glue factory or the local *ba-sashi* (raw horse meat) restaurant. The art work is mediocre but well presented. You can sit atop a plastic horse and experience the thrill of a starting gate or you can ride a horse around the video track. Remember those mechanical horses at the grocery store? The experience is the same. Visit this museum—its a sure bet.

Keiba Hakubutsukan
1-1 Hiyoshi-cho, Fuchu-shi, Tokyo
Tel: 0423-63-3141

Hours: 10:00–4:00, Wednesday–
Saturday.
9:30–4:30, Sunday.   Admission: Free.

Nankyu Softball Museum

Tobu Line from Asakusa to Kanegafuchi Station. Three-minute walk.

Baseball is Japan's most popular sport, so it was only a matter of time before softball caught on. This tiny museum stands as a public relations tool for a Tokyo company that has pioneered the manufacture and distribution of softball equipment in Japan.

The displays bear a vague resemblance to the Baseball Hall of Fame in Cooperstown, New York. Corny old pictures and autographs abound. Mixed in are photos and posters from the 1964 Tokyo Olympics.

The company official who gave us a tour was obviously proud of his company, Nagase Kenko Kabushikigaisha. "We now export softballs to America!" was one of his many boasts. He was especially proud of his company's success in New York. Pictures of former New York Mayor Ed Koch welcoming company officials seem to be the centerpiece of the collection.

Nanshiki Yakyu Shiryokan
2-36-10 Sumida, Sumida-ku, Tokyo
Tel: 3614-3501

Hours: 10:00–4:00, Monday–
Friday.
Open the same hours on the 1st and
3rd Saturday of each month.
Call to confirm.   Admission: Free.

Sumo Museum

Sobu Line to Ryogoku. Two-minute walk to main entrance of Ryogoku Kokugikan. See Map 6.

You don't have to be a sumo fan to enjoy this small museum. Located on the first floor near Ryogoku Kokugikan's main entrance, it is a delightful break after watching numerous sumo bouts. Although the explanations are in Japanese, you don't need a dictionary to appreciate many of the exhibits, such as the beautiful *keshō-mawashi,* the long decorative aprons worn by the wrestlers during their ceremonial walk about the *dohyō* (sumo ring).

Also displayed are lacquered *gunbai,* the wooden paddles with silk tassels used by famous *gyōji* (referees). Several wood-block prints adorn the walls and give the viewer a ringside seat to ancient sumo tournaments. Surprisingly, the physiques of the wrestlers have not changed over the years. For dedicated sumo fans, there are several pictures of *rikishi* (strong men), including Taiho, Takanohana, and Chiyonofuji.

Sumo Hakubutsukan
Ryogoku Kokugikan,
1-3-28 Yokoami, Sumida-ku, Tokyo
Tel: 3622-0366

Hours: 9:30–4:30, Monday–Friday
(except during sumo grand
tournaments);
ticket holders to these tournaments
are admitted while the matches are
in progress (9:00–6:00).

Admission: Free.

195

Sumo Photographic Reference Center

Sobu Line to Ryogoku, East Exit. Four-minute walk. See Map 6.

This tiny photo gallery is devoted to the glories of sumo, Japan's ancient sport. The gallery displays photos of some of the most famous *rikishi* (strong men) who have a special place in the hearts of Japanese wrestling fans. The collection includes more than 60,000 photos of *rikishi*. Only a tiny percentage of the collection is on display.

This museum is located in an unusual neighborhood, home to many of the stables that house the apprentice sumo wrestlers. Burly men in traditional dress (including topknot) walk the old streets around the museum. If you visit this museum while a sumo grand tournament is in progress, the wrestlers can be seen walking to work on the other side of the train tracks.

The Sumo Photographic Reference Center is located near the Kanto Earthquake Museum. Visit both, and allow time to absorb the atmosphere of old Sumida Ward.

Sumo Shashin Shiryokan
3-13-2 Ryogoku, Sumida-ku, Tokyo
Tel: 3631-2150

Hours: 10:00–5:00, Tuesdays.
Open every day during sumo
tournaments at nearby Ryogoku
Kokugikan.

Admission: Free.

TECHNOLOGY

技術

Communications Museum

Otemachi Station Exit A1. See Map 1.

This museum is sponsored and operated by the Ministry of Posts and Telecommunications (MPT), Nippon Telegraph and Telephone Corporation (NTT), Japan Broadcasting Corporation (NHK), and Kokusai Denshin Denwa Co. Ltd. (KDD). It is clearly designed for children. The many excited young boys running from display to display attest to its success. The first floor has displays, shops, and a snack bar. The second floor is divided between eye-catching NHK and KDD propaganda. Children will enjoy the Communications Wonderland, the NTT Time Tunnel, and the World Communication Plaza. The darkened room is full of chairs and TV terminals, each terminal recounts a chapter in NTT's history.

The third floor has an interesting set of exhibits showing the history of the Japanese postal system, as well as what has to be one of the most comprehensive stamp collections in the world. The children will go wild over the video games and various devices testing your reaction and response times to various stimuli. The lines at each terminal are quite long.

Very few of the exhibits are translated into English, but the visual, push-button nature of the displays makes translation less necessary than at other museums.

Teishin Sogo Hakubutsukan
2-3-1 Otemachi, Chiyoda-ku, Tokyo
Tel: 3244-6811

Hours: 9:00–4:30.
Closed Monday.

Admission: ¥110,
children and
high school students ¥50.

High Speed Camera Museum

Hibiya Line to Roppongi Station, Exit 2. One-minute walk. See Map 3.

The High Speed Camera Museum is located on the second floor of a new Roppongi building. The first floor is given over to displays of Hollywood history. A lifesize statue of John Wayne greets you at the door.

The second floor has yet another smashing collection of photographic artifacts. The earliest Edison machine is here, as well as its advanced Japanese progeny. The collection is particularly strong on scientific applications of photography. The best cameras used at the Kagoshima Space Center in Kyushu are tucked into one corner.

Tokyo has so many camera museums that it may be a matter for aficionados to trek around to all of them. However, the High Speed Camera Museum and the nearby Pentax Gallery have Roppongi addresses to back them up. They also have free admission, a scarce commodity in late twentieth-century Roppongi.

Eizo Gijutsu Senta
1-2-7 Nishi-Azabu, Minato-ku, Tokyo
Tel: 3403-7176

Hours: 10:30–5:00, Monday–Friday.

Admission: Free.

IBM Information-Science Museum

Otemachi Station Exit C9 is next to the museum. See Map 1.

Few things in Tokyo are free, uncrowded, and pleasant. The IBM Museum is all three. The exhibit occupies the first floor of a gleaming downtown building, and Japanese women help you work the hands-on exhibits. Mozart softly serenades you as you drift from room to room.

If you have been to many museums in Tokyo, you will be amazed at how deserted this place is. Any other place with computer terminals and electronic games would be mobbed, but the Japanese seem to steer clear of the place. This means you can play with the exhibits without fighting crowds to get to the front of the line.

The *Nihon Keizai* newspaper listed the top five companies in terms of market share in twelve key industries in Japan. IBM was the only foreign company to crack the elite sixty. The IBM museum tells the story of this unusual success, giving credit to the American, Japanese, and European scientists who made it possible. Through a microscope you can see a prototype of a 100-megabyte memory chip, scheduled for production in 1998. The exhibit is divided into an AV hall, a personal computer corner, an information library, and a science art gallery.

Ai Bi Emu Joho Kagakukan
Ote Center Building 1st Floor,
1-1-3 Otemachi, Chiyoda-ku, Tokyo
Tel: 3284-3230

Hours: 10:00–4:30.
Closed 1st, 3rd, and 4th Saturday.   Admision: Free.

200

Industrial Safety Technical Museum

Keihin Tohoku Line or Mita Line to Tamachi Station.
Two-minute walk. See Map 3.

Unless you are in the safety business or have a PhD in mechanical engineering, you can skip this museum. Located on two floors, the exhibits depict the many aspects of industrial safety. There are displays of fire-retardant jumpsuits, safety goggles, and shock-proof rubber boots to round out the attire of a safety-conscious worker. Even the ascent up the staircase to the second floor is educational, with illustrations telling you how wide the stairs should be.

There are displays of machine guards, automatic turn off switches, and other safety measures that should be used to keep industrial accidents to a minimum. Surprisingly (thankfully) there are no industrial accident photographs; such gruesome pictorials are reserved for the *manga* (violent comic books popular in Japan). The Minato Ward museum is only a few blocks away so a visit to both is easy.

Kigyo Anzen Gijutsukan
5-35-1 Shiba, Minato-ku, Tokyo
Tel: 3453-8441

Hours: 9:30–4:00, Monday–Friday.　　　　　　Admission: Free.

201

JCII Camera Museum

Hanzomon Line to Hanzomon Station, Exit 4. Two-minute walk.
See Map 1.

This museum is a must for photography buffs. The museum is located in the basement of the Japan Camera Institute next to the Diamond Hotel. You can see one of the largest collections of cameras in Asia, as well as learn about the history of the Japanese camera industry.

One of the unusual displays shows a cutaway view of the modern single lens reflex camera, along with all components that are assembled into the amazing machine. You can see spy cameras encased in cigarette lighters, clunky old box cameras, and the high-tech new breeds from the gods of Nikon.

Many classic cameras are also on display. Bronica, Hasselblad, Rollei, and Mamiya classics are in abundance, as well as a huge display of Soviet cameras. The collection lacks representatives of the Graphlex and early Kodak era, but, after all, no museum is perfect.

The curator, an old camera buff, speaks excellent English and likes to chat with foreign visitors. The English handout, *The Evolution of the Japanese Camera*, is written in impeccable academic prose. The essay is candid, and attributes the success of the Japanese camera industry to "evolution rather than innovation."

Nihon Kamera Hakubutsukan
JCII Ichibancho Building,
25 Ichibancho, Chiyoda-ku, Tokyo
Tel: 3263-7110

Hours: 10:00–5:00.
Closed Monday. Open if Monday is
a holiday, then closed on Tuesday.

Admission: ¥300.

Konica Plaza Camera Museum

Marunouchi Line to Shinjuku-Sanchome Station, Exit B13.
See Map 5.

If you are wandering around the action-packed area near Shinjuku Station's East Exit, and decide you need a bit of peace and quiet, head for this museum. It is located on the fourth floor of a building next to the huge movie screen that looms over Shinjuku. The small interior houses temporary photographic displays, a camera museum, and a camera library. A pert OL (uniformed office lady) presides over the festivities.

Camera fans will love the place, even though the collection pales compared to the JCII Camera Museum in Hanzomon. The Konica collection is particularly strong in miniature cameras, including Minox, Konica, and Soviet varieties. The displays also include old Japanese film and photo accessories. Considering the financial interest that Konica has in pumping its products in this high rent district, the displays are surprisingly fair and uncommercialized.

Visitors should avail themselves of the free postcards commemorating the temporary exhibits. Sit down and look at the photos before descending into the maelstrom of Shinjuku.

Konica Puraza
3-24-2 Shinjuku, Shinjuku-ku, Tokyo
Tel: 3225-5001

Hours: 10:00–7:00.   Admission: Free.

203

NHK Broadcast Museum

Hibiya Line to Kamiyacho Station. Ten-minute walk. See Map 3.

This museum traces the history of radio and television broadcasting in Japan. Memorabilia fans will like this place. You can see hoary radios and antique speakers. Beethoven's *Fifth Symphony* serenades you as you walk up the stairs. You can switch the music from modern Sony speakers to the antique Victor gramophone horn. The quality of the sound is surprisingly similar.

The second floor has several television monitors showing great events in Japan's history. State visits by foreign leaders and Sadaharu Oh's home-run to break Hank Aaron's record figure prominently in the iconography. You can also visit mockups of the earliest broadcasting studios as well as the new ones used by NHK. One exhibit allows you to sit in mock bullet-train seats next to a blank blue screen. When you look up at the television monitor above, you can see the scenery pass by your "window." This is how those melodrama scenes on Japanese television are filmed.

One thing you should not miss is the beautiful Shinto shrine next door to the main entrance. It is one of the most exquisite shrines in all of Tokyo, and provides a bit of peace and solitude.

NHK Hoso Hakubutsukan
2-1-1 Atago, Minato-ku, Tokyo
Tel: 3433-5211

Hours: 9:30–4:30.
Closed Monday.

Admission: Free.

Pentax Museum

Hibiya Line to Roppongi Station. Seven-minute walk. See Map 3.

Swinging Roppongi is better known for its bars and call girls than cultural institutions, but the Pentax Museum is doing its bit to change this image. This sleepy little museum is on the second floor of a building surrounded by billion yen boutiques. The museum is operated by the Asahi Pentax Corporation, but has a superb collection of antique cameras by other makers. There are at least a hundred old Kodaks on display, as well as French, English, and Soviet cameras.

The guest register documents only two or three visitors a day, so the museum hardly suffers from overexposure. It is a pity, because the collection is in the same league as competing camera museums, Konica Plaza in Shinjuku, and the JCII Camera Museum in Hanzomon. The Pentax Museum is hardly a must-see, but it is worth a visit if you are a camera buff, or need some peace and quiet in Roppongi.

Pentakkusu Gyarari Kamera Hakubutsukan
3-21-20 Nishi-Azabu, Minatu-ku, Tokyo
Tel: 3401-2186

Hours: 10:00–5:00.
Closed Sunday.   Admission: Free.

205

Tokyo Electric Ikebukuro Service Center

Yamanote Line or other train to Ikebukuro Station, West Exit.
Five-minute walk.

This little museum has a collection of materials from the days when Tokyo first started using electric power. It is located on the second floor of a TEPCO (Tokyo Electric Power Company) office in Ikebukuro.

The collection starts with essentials, such as the earliest electric rice-cookers, and moves on to early television sets, radios, and air conditioners. The displays are a bit dusty, reminiscent of those broken appliances stored in your garage.

A nearby room allows local artists to display their paintings for a short period of time. If you get tired of looking at the old appliances, you can take a break and look at some new art.

Tokyo Denryoku Ikebukuro Sabisu Senta Shiryoshitsu
1-8-9 Higashi-Ikebukuro, Toshima-ku, Tokyo
Tel: 3971-0809

Hours: 9:00–5:00.
Closed Saturday and Sunday.   Admission: Free.

TEMPORARY DISPLAYS

巡回展示場

Azabu Museum of Arts and Crafts

Hibiya Line to Roppongi Station, Exit A4. Five-minute walk.
See Map 3.

The Azabu Museum is another product of the bubble economy whereby Japan suddenly became the richest nation in the world with the assistance of the rapid appreciation of the yen, as well as other factors. Tokyo now has many spectacular museum buildings without permanent collections worthy of the surroundings. The Azabu Museum fits into this category.

The Azabu Museum is near plastic, fantastic Roppongi Crossing, and occupies the first three floors of a futuristic glass-and-steel building. The museum opened in 1989, and provides a home to various traveling exhibits from Europe and other parts of the world.

The first floor has a splendid gift shop and a cafe. The cafe is magnificent even by the high standards of Tokyo museum cafes. It is easy to forget you are in tawdry Roppongi while sitting on furniture looking out onto a peaceful neighborhood scene. One of the last traditional homes in all of Roppongi looms outside the floor-to-ceiling window. The second floor has a small video display area, and dark exhibition areas with brightly lit glass cases. The third floor is more of the same.

Azabu Bijutsu Kogeikan
4-6-9 Roppongi, Minato-ku, Tokyo
Tel: 5474-1371

Hours: 11:00–7:00.
Closed Monday.

Admission: Varies; maximum ¥900,
¥700 for student.

Bunkamura Museum

Ginza, Yamanote or other line to Shibuya Station. Seven-minute walk. See Map 4.

The Bunkamura complex is the crown jewel of the Tokyu group. Bunkamura houses a concert hall patterned after Avery Fisher Hall in New York City, an art-movie theater, an art bookstore, and a museum. Any concert hall that commemorates its opening by importing the entire Bayreuth Festival Opera Company, as Bunkamura did in 1989, clearly has delusions of grandeur.

The Bunkamura Museum is not in this league. Located in the lower level of the spectacular complex, the museum houses various temporary exhibits. So far, it has not attracted first rate exhibits such as those garnered by Isetan. The relatively high admission price makes the museum a secondary destination for someone coming to Bunkamura for a concert. It is one of the most pleasant places in Tokyo to enjoy classical music, so the museum may be worth a visit if you have time to kill before the concert.

Another bet would be a drink or a snack at the adjacent Les Deux Magots cafe, which provides Franco-Japanese ambience at its best.

Bunkamura Bijutsukan
2-24-1 Dogenzaka, Shibuya-ku, Tokyo
Tel: 3477-3244

Hours: 10:00–7:00.
Friday and Saturday until 9:00.
Closed Monday.

Admission: ¥1000,
primary and
middle school students, ¥500.

209

Daimaru Museum

JR to Tokyo Station, Yaesu Central Exit. Three-minute walk.
See Map 1.

If you have a spare half hour waiting for a connection with Tokyo's JR Railway network, go to the Daimaru Department Store and wander through its food halls or its museum. The exhibits are not as grand as those at Isetan or Takashimaya, but you won't have to fight the crowds to see the art. The exhibits are first rate and have included photographs by Meltzer and paintings by Millet. If a famous artist is not featured, Tokyo's masses stay away even in crowded Tokyo Station. Present your ticket to gain admittance and you get a discount coupon for the next exhibit.

Avoid the smoke-filled and noisy train platforms and wait for your train at Daimaru. On your way out, stop at the food hall in the basement and buy a snack for the ride.

Daimaru Myujiamu
1-9-1 Marunouchi, Chiyoda-ku, Tokyo
Tel: 3212-8011

Hours: 10:00–7:00.
Closed Wednesday.

Admission: ¥800,
¥600 for university and high school
students, ¥400 for middle and
primary school students.
(Prices can vary with exhibits.)

Isetan Museum

JR trains to Shinjuku East Exit (three minute-walk) or Marunouchi subway to Shinjuku-Sanchome Station, Exit B2. See Map 5.

Most of Tokyo's ritzy department stores have art museums. These art museums host traveling exhibits from around the world. All of the department stores get good exhibits, but Isetan has the best.

We have been to at least twenty different exhibits at Isetan, and have yet to see a bad one. There has been extraordinary diversity to the art displayed at this cozy little museum, from Bracque to Lichtenstien. The best exhibits have been traveling exhibits from the Bellas Artes Museum in Buenos Aires and the Hartford Museum in the United States.

The exhibits are temporary and last usually three weeks. Isetan advertises heavily; anyone who rides the subway can see the ads near the ceiling, proudly trumpeting the latest show.

A visit to Isetan is one of Tokyo's best free shows. The lively food stalls in the basement, patterned after Harrod's in London, are always interesting. No other department store in the world surpasses Isetan in style, and no department store has a better museum.

Isetan Bijutsukan
3-14-1 Shinjuku, Shinjuku-ku, Tokyo
Tel: 3352-1111

Hours: 10:00–7:00.
Closed Wednesday.

Admission: ¥500–¥1000 (average is ¥700).
Free if you are a foreign resident—register with the Isetan Foreign Buyer's Club and request free tickets.

Itabashi Art Museum

Mita Line to Nishi-Takashimadaira Station (end of line).
Seven-minute walk.

This museum is only worth a visit for two reasons: If you are visiting the wonderful Itabashi Historical Museum, which is part of the same park/museum complex, or you are like us, and want to go to every museum in Tokyo. Only the hard-core would otherwise venture this far for so little.

The Itabashi Art Museum is housed in a white building that resembles a high school fieldhouse with a modern slanted design. The interior gives shelter to various traveling exhibits. Whether or not you like the exhibit, you will probably find the setting disappointing. The art work is hung on dirty walls in a dingy room on the second floor. You wonder if you are in a museum or a warehouse.

The only saving grace is the lounge area on the first floor which displays posters of exhibitions at other museums around Tokyo. The concept is not unique to Itabashi, but it is particularly well done.

Itabashi Bijutsukan
5-34-27 Akatsuka, Itabashi-ku, Tokyo
Tel: 3977-1000

Hours: 9:00–4:00.   Admission: Free.

212

LaForet Museum

Hibiya Line to Kamiyacho Station. Five-minute walk. See Map 3.

The LaForet Museum is more a gallery than a museum, but we will call the noble building the name it prefers to be called. This modern building looks more like an office block than a museum, but there is plenty of windowless display space inside. There is no permanent exhibition, and the vagabond exhibits which find their way here range from the sublime to the ridiculous.

Our last visit found an interesting exhibit of folk crafts from Yamagata Prefecture, including small samples of saké and food. Other visits have found the place off-limits due to invitation-only special events.

The proximity of the museum to Tokyo Tower, the American Club, and various other downtown destinations, make the museum a worthwhile place to drop in on a rainy Sunday afternoon, but you need not go out of your way to visit this one.

Rafore Myujiamu
Mori Building 39, 2-4-5 Azabu-dai, Minato-ku, Tokyo
Tel: 3433-6801

Hours: vary with exhibit.   Admission: varies with exhibit.

Meguro Museum of Art

Yamanote Line to Meguro Station West Exit. Ten-minute walk.
See Map 4.

The Meguro Museum of Art is one of the most beautiful museums in Japan. The museum spans three ultramodern stories, and has a spacious feeling that makes it a wonderful place to spend an afternoon. However, it lacks a permanent collection worth talking about. Until a permanent collection is assembled, the curators have to scratch around for traveling exhibits. For that reason, you can often find unusual exhibitions here. Nothing has come close to the spectacular impressionist exhibit of 1988, but the exhibits are always interesting and tastefully presented.

The basement houses the Kumin Gallery, and features sliding walls accommodating a variety of local exhibits, including an occasional display of children's art. The first floor has a splendid cafe with a beautiful view of the grounds through floor-to-ceiling windows. It is almost worth the ¥500 admission price just to have a coffee in such a tranquil setting. The second floor houses the visiting collection, which can be excellent or pedestrian. It is better to call ahead or read the local press to see if the exhibit is worth the trip.

Meguro Bijutsukan
2-4-36 Meguro, Meguro-ku, Tokyo
Tel: 3714-1201

Hours: 10:00–6:00.

Admission: ¥900,
¥700 for high school and college students, ¥500 for primary and middle school students.

Mori Museum

*Yamanote Line, Ginza Line, or Keisei Line to Ueno Station.
Ten-minute walk from any exit, but Koen Exit to the Bunka Kaikan
is the quickest.*

This museum was opened in 1972, and is within easy walking distance of the many tourist attractions in Ueno Park. The museum is modern and bright, but it does not have a permanent collection of note. You may find a fine traveling exhibit, or a boring amateur exhibit. This is one museum where it pays to call ahead to see what is on display.

The Mori Museum has the obligatory coffee shop and gift shop, and a second floor that is opened if the exhibit justifies the space. This is often the case when the museum has an exhibition of amateur or semiprofessional artists. The Mori Museum is worth a visit if you are strolling in Ueno Park and want to check out yet another splendid building in search of a collection. Other than that, you can avoid it.

Mori Bijutsukan
1-2 Ueno Koen, Koto-ku, Tokyo
Tel: 3833-4191

Admission: Free.
(Special exhibits require a
small charge.)

Hours: 10:00–5:00.

O Art Museum

Yamanote Line to Osaki Station, East Exit. Two-minute walk.

The O Art Museum sports a concept that could catch on—a shopping center museum. Located on the second floor of a glittering, sprawling mall, the museum looks like just another boutique or pretty restaurant until you get close.

Unfortunately, location is only one of the factors in the decision to visit a museum. The museum must have something worth seeing to make you want to go there in the first place. On this score, the O Museum fails the test. So far, it is dependent on temporary exhibitions, and it has not been able to attract stellar material to fill its shelves.

Our negative impressions are to some extent based on the orientation of the museum toward contemporary Japanese art. This is not one of our favorite art forms, and an exhibit has to be truly superior to make a good impression. Truly superior collections are scarce, and the O Museum has not attracted them.

The high price is another disadvantage—¥500 for a museum that is the size of a decent apartment. It is rare for us to leave a museum feeling that the admission price would have been better spent at a nearby noodle restaurant.

O Bijutsukan
Osaki New City, 1-6-2 Osaki, Shinagawa-ku, Tokyo
Tel: 3495-4040

Hours: 10:00–6:30.
Closed Thursday.

Admission: Varies; maximum ¥500,
¥300 for university students,
¥100 for younger students and
children.

Sogo Museum of Art

JR to Yokohama Station. Three-minute walk.

The Sogo Department store in Yokohama is one of the largest such stores in all of Japan. On Saturday afternoons, it seems like half of the population of Yokohama has attempted to enter the store. Fortunately, Sogo has a quiet place to rest—the Sogo Museum of Art.

The museum has no permanent collection, but Sogo has been able to consistently attract quality exhibitions. Particularly memorable was the collection from the Belgrade National Museum in 1991. Sogo has also hosted excellent retrospectives on leading Japanese artists.

Sogo Bijutsukan
2-18-1 Takashima, Nishi-ku, Yokohama
Tel: 045-465-2361

Hours: 10:00–6:30.
Closed Tuesday.

Admission: ¥800,
¥600 for students.

217

Striped House Museum of Art

Hibiya Line to Roppongi Station, exits for Roppongi Crossing and Almond. Five-minute walk. See Map 3.

If you are interested in avant-garde sculpture, the Striped House Museum should not be missed. The museum occupies the basement and three floors of a small modern building, with tan and white stripes, in the heart of neon-lit Roppongi. The exhibition changes every month, but you can expect to see about twenty of the most far-out works you can imagine. The atmosphere is more like a modern art gallery than a museum, but the proprietors insist it is a proper museum. It is their business to call it what they like.

Our visit yielded views of a fluted sculpture filled with live bees, a mechanical gong player, and dangling mobiles straight out of Calder's nightmares. The modern surroundings, inside and outside the museum, suit the adventurous displays.

The Striped House Museum has a small but unusually good bookstore, selling numerous books about modern art that you will be hard-pressed to find elsewhere. There is plenty to do in and near Roppongi, and a visit to the Striped House can be combined with a visit to the Azabu Museum on the opposite side of Roppongi Crossing.

Sutoraipu Hausu Bijutsukan
5-10-33 Roppongi, Tokyo
Tel: 3405-8108

Hours: 11:00–6:30.
Closed Sundays and Holidays.   Admission: Free.

218

Tokyo Station Gallery

Numerous trains to Tokyo Station, Marunouchi North or South exits.
See Map 1.

In most countries, the main train station is a bit seedy, dere-licts abound and the place needs a good scrubbing. In Japan, a nation trying to be recognized as number one in everything, some of its train stations are works of art. The crown jewel of Japan's train stations, Tokyo Station, even has its own art museum.

Tokyo Station Gallery resembles a nice urban loft. Exposed brick and modern furnishings abound. The Gallery usually shows traveling exhibitions. The lack of exhibition space makes small collections a must.

Millions of people travel through Tokyo Station without ever giving the gallery a look. Occasionally a hot exhibit such as the Picasso exhibit in 1988 will pack the place, but this is a rare event. If you have occasion to be in Marunouchi, or you are a train station buff, give the gallery a try. Otherwise, call ahead to see if the exhibition interests you.

Tokyo-Eki Hakubutsukan
1-9-1 Marunouchi, Chiyoda-ku, Tokyo
Tel: 3212-2485

Hours: 10:00–7:30.
Closed Monday.

Admission: ¥500,
¥400 for students.

Watari Contemporary Museum of Art

Ginza Line to Gaienmae Station. Eight-minute walk.

Modern art museums sprout like weeds in Tokyo, but the Watari Museum is so well done that it is a cut or two above the competition. The futuristic concrete-and-glass building was completed in 1989, and is on a street packed with boutiques and swanky art galleries. The top three floors of the museum are reserved for the latest and strangest from the world of art. The exhibitions change seasonally. The Watari Museum sponsors lectures and other activities and encourages foreigners to attend.

The first floor is occupied by an art materials store selling all kinds of brushes, postcards, and posters. The basement has one of the best art bookstores in all of Tokyo, in some ways even better than the famous bookstore in the Bunkamura complex in Shibuya. The bookstore has a tiny cafe that serves cof-

Watari-Um
3-7-6 Jingumae, Shibuya-ku, Tokyo
Tel: 3402-3001

Hours: 11:00–7:00.
Closed Monday.

Admission: ¥800,
¥600 for students.

TOYS

玩具

Japan Toy Museum

Ginza Line to Asakusa Station, Exit 5. Bus #7 to Senju
Kiyokawa-Nichome, or Hashiba-Nichome if the bus goes this far.
Ten-minute walk from Senju Kiyokawa-Nichome or two-minute walk
from Hashiba-Nichome stop. See Map 2.

Godzilla greets you when you visit this museum. It is clearly Tokyo's best toy museum, and there are toys that will please visitors of all ages. Remember those cheap tin metal cars, buses, fire engines, and action figures? The collection at this museum is awesome. The toys are crammed into glass wall-displays which do not do the collection justice. It is hard to appreciate an individual toy since it is thrown in together with hundreds of other toys—like your old toy box.

The two floors are small, but there are so many toys you could spend several hours there. As you go down memory lane and see toys that you had long forgotten about, there are video games that allow the younger generation to amuse themselves. Unfortunately these games rather than the stuffed animals, board games, and kites seem to be the kids' favorite. For train buffs there is a decent train set that you can operate. On the seventh floor there is a lovely patio which overlooks the Sumida River and a refreshment bar with travel photographs.

Nihon Gangu Shiryokan
Tsukuda Group Bldg., 1-36-10 Hashiba, Taito-ku, Tokyo
Tel: 3874-5133

Hours: 9:30–5:00.
Closed Monday.

Admission: ¥200,
¥100 for children.

Kobayashi Doll Museum

Keisei Oshiage Line from Asakusa to Arakawa Station. Seven-minute walk.

A tiny doll museum in Sumida Ward is the last place you would expect to find ghosts from World War II. Old man Kobayashi has turned the second floor of his humble abode into a doll museum. You wend your way through the junk and barking dogs and squeeze into the back door. Kobayashi will drag you upstairs to show you his pride and joy.

In 1927, primary schools in the US and Japan exchanged dolls as an act of friendship. Dr. Sidney Gulick supervised the shipment of 13,000 blue-eyed dolls to Yokohama. When Japanese-American relations soured in the 1930s, nearly all of the American dolls were destroyed in public hate ceremonies. The Yokohama Doll Museum has an example of the American dolls but only Kobayashi has specimens from both sides of the Pacific.

It is an odd feeling, silently looking at press reports of the doll-bashing incident, as well as the two surviving dolls. The splendid Sachiko, clad in a beautiful kimono, stands next to her blue-eyed American sister. Kobayashi gives you a candid, nonstop commentary on the dolls and the odd incident that caused their demise.

Kobayashi Ningyo Shiryokan
6-31-2 Ya Hiro, Sumida-ku, Tokyo
Tel: 3612-1644

Hours: 10:00–5:00,
Friday, Saturday, and Sunday.   Admission: Free.

Murai Playing Card Museum

Inokashira Line from Eifukucho Station. Six-minute walk. Also walking distance from Honancho Station on the Marunouchi Line.

Mr. Murai is an old man living in a small house in Suginami Ward. His street and house are like millions of others in Japan. However, Murai has distinguished himself from his neighbors by converting a tiny room in his house into a museum housing his pride and joy: a wonderful collection of playing cards.

Portuguese traders introduced *karuta* (playing cards) into Japan prior to the period of seclusion. Japan's dictators tried to eradicate the foreign perversion, but were not successful. The Japanese love a game of chance as much as anyone else. Soon, the Japanese were producing playing cards on their own. Hokusai, one of the masters of the woodblock print, created a set of playing cards. The Hokusai cards are among the finest artifacts in Murai's collection.

Murai will greet you in slacks and a sporty beret. He is delighted to have foreign visitors; they come every couple of years or so.

Murai Karuta Shiryokan
4-32-22 Eifuku, Suginami-ku, Tokyo
Tel: 3322-1408

Hours: 10:30–5:30.
Closed Monday.

Admission: ¥400,
¥200 for children.

Tokyo Metropolitan Children's Hall

Yamanote Line or subway to Shibuya East Exit. Seven-minute walk.
See Map 4.

Many Tokyo museums purport to serve the children of Tokyo. This one delivers on its promise. The Children's Hall sprawls over five floors, as well as having play areas on the roof and in the basement. The rooms contain virtually every kind of display and scientific toy to keep your children out of your hair—for a few minutes.

Particularly remarkable is the Art and Music Center which occupies most of the fourth floor. Various rooms offer opportunities for listening, doodling, painting, and making woodblock prints. The place is so chaotic that most people don't pay attention to foreigners.

Interesting, but sobering, is the Amusement, Craft, and Exhibition Center in the basement. Little boys are eagerly sculpting woodwork with fast-spinning saws. This place must have its share of horrible accidents. Another room in the basement allows kids to drive around in little cars for ¥100. This appears safe, and fulfills the dreams of every little boy and girl to drive their own car.

Tokyo-to Jidokan
1-18-24 Shibuya, Shibuya-ku, Tokyo
Tel: 3409-6361

Hours: 9:00–5:00.
Closed different days each month;
call to confirm.

Admission: Free.

225

Toy Museum

Chuo Line to Nakano Station. Fifteen-minute walk.

Overpriced but interesting, the Toy Museum occupies the second, third, and fourth floors above a small toy store in Nakano Ward. The second floor has a playroom where children can play with modern items like tabletop soccer and stuffed bears. However, most of the floor consists of small toys behind glass displays so you can look but can't touch. The Chinese, Mongolian, and English dolls are worth lingering over.

The third floor features a live puppet show. The little ones (and bigger visitors) perch on small chairs and watch the show. The puppets peer out over the top of an enclosed room, carrying on a dialogue with the audience and an adult assistant. It does not take much Japanese to understand the show. The third floor is also the place to go for hands-on activities for the children. Marker coloring, cutouts, and sketch pads are all available at the small desk. The children flock there before and after the puppet display.

Very few of the exhibits are collectors items. Adults who expect the detail, value, and beautiful presentation that is common in Japanese museums will be disappointed. If you bring kids, rush them through the shop on the first floor and head for the higher floors. The ¥500 admission price is cheaper than buying souvenirs to take home.

Omocha Bijutsukan
2-12-10 Arai, Nakano-ku, Tokyo
Tel: 3387-5461

Hours: 10:30–5:00.
Closed Friday.

Admission: ¥500.

Toys Club Museum

Bus #11 from Sakuragicho Station. Three-minute walk.

Don't be fooled by the entrance—the toy store really does have a small museum in the back room. It may be hard to steer the kids away from the merchandise to the museum but unless they are interested in old tin toys don't bother. The owner, Mr. Kitahara, has amassed a fine collection of old tin fire trucks, race cars, and motorcycles. There is even a huge Godzilla hiding in a corner ready to spring out. The collection is in excellent condition and authentic except for the merry-go-round horses in the back yard. There are two buildings next door which sell clothing and Christmas decorations. The prices are hefty but 'tis the season . . .

Buriki no Omocha Hakubutsukan
239 Yamatecho, Naka-ku, Yokohama
Tel: 045-621-8710

Hours: 10:00–5:00.

Admission: ¥200,
¥100 for children.

Yokohama Doll Museum

Bus from Sakuragicho Station to Yamashitacho. Five-minute walk.

This is the only museum in Yokohama that screams commercialism! The doll collection is excellent, if you can ignore the hype and the revolving doll displays. Don't forget to ask for the English brochure which gives a nice explanation of the history of the museum. The entrance fee is a bit steep but the museum will delight children—especially little girls. There is even a puppet show on the top floor.

The collection consists of dolls from all over the world. There are dolls from Africa, Turkey, and Nepal. Don't miss the "friendship" dolls given by the US to Japanese children in 1927. These dolls are very rare since the little tykes were forced to destroy their dolls in public hate ceremonies when the militarists seized control of Japan. The Japanese doll collection from the Edo, Meiji, Taisho, and Showa eras is massive as well as beautiful.

Yokohama Ningyo no Ie
18 Banchi Yamashitacho, Naka-ku, Yokohama
Tel: 045-671-9361

Hours: 10:00–5:00.
Closed Monday.

Admission: ¥300,
¥150 for primary school and
middle school students.

228

TRANSPORT

交通

Hikawa Maru

Bus #8 from Sakuragicho Station to Yamashita Park stop.
Three-minute walk.

The Hikawa Maru is a luxury ocean liner that has retired to the friendly confines of Yokohama Harbor. The interior of the ship has been restored with great attention to detail. The travel books in the ship's library during the 1930s are displayed under glass. The infirmary is primed and ready to treat patients.

Boat buffs could spend hours on the ship, but thirty minutes is enough time to get a flavor of the ocean-going experience. Audiovisual displays appear in every corner, simulating the sounds and sights of being at sea. One room was converted to simulate the ship's deck at night, complete with seagulls and star display.

The boat is located in a lively area of Yokohama, near the Doll Museum and the Silk Museum, as well as many other tourist attractions. Yokohama is one of the best day trips out of Tokyo, and the Hikawa Maru should not be missed.

Hikawa Maru
Yamashita Koen, Yamashitacho, Naka-ku, Yokohama
Tel: 045-641-4361

Admission: ¥800,
¥400 for children, primary and
middle school students.

Hours: 10:00–5:00.

230

Nippon Express Museum

JR lines to Akihabara, Exit for Department Store. Two-minute walk.
See Map 1.

Located in the heart of Akihabara, the electric capital of the world, this museum does not have one electric computer, video display, or anything that lights up. Indeed, we were beginning to think that electronic gadgetry was obligatory for Tokyo's museums. Ironically, Nippon Express most likely transported many of the electronic goods found throughout the neighborhood.

Don't let the loud elevator music blasting through the tiny one-room museum shorten your stay—you can see the whole place in ten minutes. Nothing is in English, but the wood-block prints, old wooden signs, truck and ship models, and uniforms are mildly interesting. The company can be traced back to 1664, and was affiliated with the government until the postwar period when it finally became private. Unless you are particularly interested in Japan's transportation industry, or you are looking for something free to do in the area, skip this one.

Nippon Tsuun Shiryokan
Nippon Express Bldg.,
4th floor, 3-12-9 Soto-Kanda, Chiyoda-ku, Tokyo
Tel: 3253-1111

Hours: 10:00–4:00 Monday–Friday,
but closed 12:00–1:00.   Admission: Free.

231

Subway Museum

Tozai Line to Kasai Station. Directly in front of the subway station.

The Subway Museum will please train freaks, the curious, and little boys, not necessarily in that order. The Tokyo Metropolitan Transit System is so intent on plugging the museum that they announce it on the Tozai Line loudspeaker system as the train pulls into the station. The Subway Museum spans 35,985 square meters, and was completed in 1986. Although the museum purports to depict the history of subways, the display begins with the history of Japanese subways, ignoring the history that preceded the Asakusa to Ueno line in 1927. The thousands of children visiting this museum must think that the technology originated in Tokyo, rather than Budapest or London.

Insularity aside, this is a good museum. You pass through an automatic subway ticket-gate to enter the museum, and then pass through a nostalgic hall showing the earliest subway lines complete with kimono-clad ticket takers.

More interesting are the hands-on exhibits showing the little ones how they can drive a subway car. Retired transit men guide the drivers through the intricate steps of stopping each subway train on a dime. The lifelike audiovisual system gives you a feel for the madness you experience every morning.

Chikatetsu Hakubutsukan
6-3-1 Higashi-Kasai, Edogawa-ku, Tokyo
Tel: 3878-5011

Hours: 10:00–5:00.
Closed Monday.

Admission: ¥200,
¥100 for children.

Tobu Museum of Transport and Culture

Tobu Line from Asakusa to Higashi-Mukojima. Thirty-second walk.

Like the Transportation Museum and the Subway Museum, the displays of old trains, mock railcars, train axles, gears, and driver simulators, give the visitor a feeling of déjà vu. You can find this museum quite easily since it is located within the Higashi-Mukojima Station. Purchasing your admission ticket in the ticket machine can be as confusing as buying a train ticket.

There are several old photographs that depict the station houses along the Tobu Line and the maps on the walls show the history and expansion of the Tobu Line throughout the decades. The building is new, the bathrooms spotless (unlike the Tobu stations) and the scheduled movies do run on time (like the Tobu trains). The museum is not as crowded as the other transportation museums but it is a little out of the way—especially if you follow the curator's travel directions (Tobu Line all the way).

Tobu Hakubutsukan
4-28-16 Higashi-Mukojima, Sumida-ku, Tokyo
Tel: 3614-8811

Hours: 10:00–4:00.
Closed Monday.

Admission: ¥200,
¥100 for children.

Transportation Museum

JR Akihabara, Ochanomizu, and Kanda Station, five-to-twelve minute walk; subway Awajicho, Kanda, Ogawamachi, and Shin-Ochanomizu Station, four-to-twelve-minute walk. See Map 1.

The Transportation Museum is another children's museum with more than enough to keep the adults entertained. It is noteworthy because it combines some of the elements of the Subway Museum and the Bicycle Culture Center under one roof.

Train buffs will love this museum. Old steam locomotives have laid claim to the first floor, while mock passenger cars and control panels are on the second floor. Even the inexpensive cafeteria on the fourth floor is an exact replica of a train dining car.

Planes are also represented in this museum. There is a life-size mockup of a Japan Airlines Boeing passenger cabin, as well as miniature warplanes from World War II.

Even if you are too tight to spend ¥260, you can see an old train car from Hokkaido. It occupies a place of honor in the front yard next to the entrance. There are plenty of other free sights in the area, including the Russian Orthodox Nikolai Cathedral and the electronic wonderland, Akihabara.

Kotsu Hakubutsukan
1-25 Kanda Sudacho, Chiyoda-ku, Tokyo
Tel: 3251-7025

Hours: 9:30–5:00.

Admission: ¥260,
¥150 for children.

Yohohama Maritime Museum

JR to Sakuragicho Station. Seven-minute walk.

If Captain Bligh turned into a yuppie and drove a BMW, he would park it in front of this museum. Yokohama's harbor, once a rough and ready place, has come of age. The city has poured money into developing the harbor, and the Maritime Museum is one of the centerpieces of this effort.

The museum oozes affluence, from the parquet floors to the dozens of color television monitors. Displays include the predictable, such as Yokohama's history, paths of Japanese exports, and techniques for tying sailors' knots. The unpredictable displays include a series of old movie posters involving movies based on maritime themes.

There is a small quay in front of the museum which is the home of a training ship for Japanese shipping companies. Admission to the museum allows you to climb aboard and explore the ship. The boat is not as grand as the Hikaru Maru one kilometer away, but it is interesting in its own right.

Yokohama Maritaimu Myujiamu
2-1-1 Minatomirai, Nishi-ku, Yokohama
Tel: 045-221-0280

Hours: 10:00–5:00;
until 4:30 during November and
December;
6:30 during July and August.
Closed Monday.

Admission: ¥400,
¥200 for children.

235

Yokohama Trolley Car Museum

JR lines to Negishi Station. Five-minute walk.

This museum is a must for nostalgia fans. For others, it is a bit of a disappointment. The museum chronicles the days when Yokohama and other Japanese cities were served by clanging trolley cars. The museum houses some of the original trolley cars, and has other items, such as old maps of the trolley routes.

Children will enjoy working the simulator, which gives them an idea of what it is like to be in the driver's seat of one of these vehicles. The museum is off the beaten track, located far from most of Yokohama's other museums. Only the hard core will think that it is worth the effort it takes to get to the museum.

Yokohama Shiden Hozonkan
3-1-53 Takigashira, Isogu-ku, Yokohama
Tel: 045-751-9625

Hours: 10:00–4:00.
Closed Monday.

Admission: ¥200,
¥100 for children.

MAPS

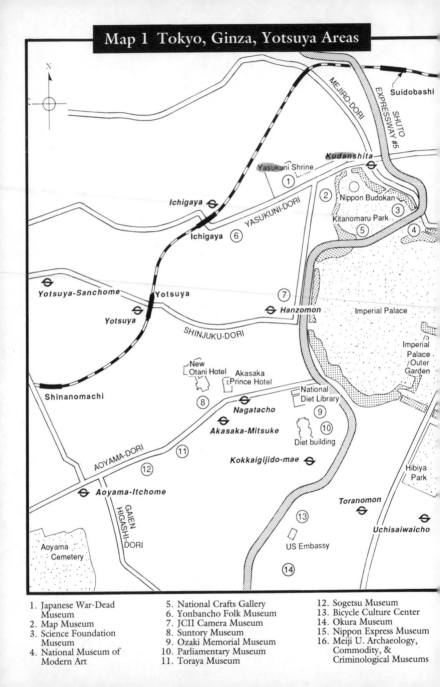

Map 1 Tokyo, Ginza, Yotsuya Areas

1. Japanese War-Dead Museum
2. Map Museum
3. Science Foundation Museum
4. National Museum of Modern Art
5. National Crafts Gallery
6. Yonbancho Folk Museum
7. JCII Camera Museum
8. Suntory Museum
9. Ozaki Memorial Museum
10. Parliamentary Museum
11. Toraya Museum
12. Sogetsu Museum
13. Bicycle Culture Center
14. Okura Museum
15. Nippon Express Museum
16. Meiji U. Archaeology, Commodity, & Criminological Museums

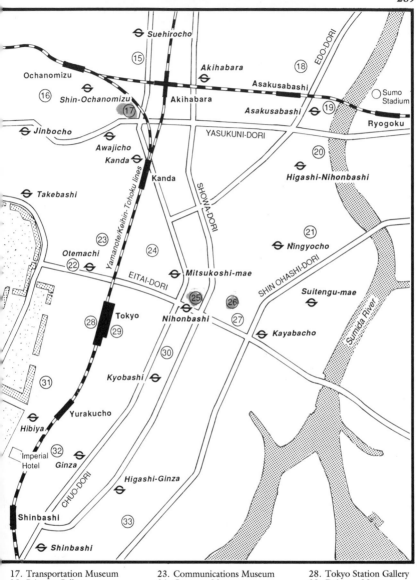

17. Transportation Museum
18. Princess Gallery
19. Stationery Museum
20. Button Museum
21. Kurita Museum
22. IBM Information-Science Museum
23. Communications Museum
24. Currency Museum
25. Kite Museum
26. Stock Market Museum
27. Yamatane Museum
28. Tokyo Station Gallery
29. Daimaru Museum
30. Bridgestone Museum
31. Idemitsu Museum
32. Riccar Museum
33. Tsukiji Ward Museum

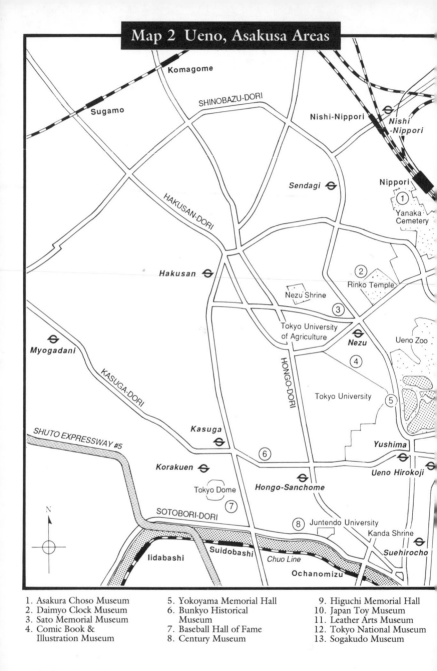

Map 2 Ueno, Asakusa Areas

Komagome

SHINOBAZU-DORI

Sugamo

Nishi-Nippori

Nishi-Nippori

Sendagi

Nippori

HAKUSAN-DORI

Yanaka Cemetery

Hakusan

Rinko Temple

Nezu Shrine

Myogadani

Tokyo University of Agriculture

Nezu

Ueno Zoo

KASUGA-DORI

HONGO-DORI

Tokyo University

SHUTO EXPRESSWAY #5

Kasuga

Yushima

Korakuen

Ueno Hirokoji

Tokyo Dome

Hongo-Sanchome

SOTOBORI-DORI

Juntendo University

Kanda Shrine

Iidabashi

Suidobashi

Chuo Line

Suehirocho

N

Ochanomizu

1. Asakura Choso Museum
2. Daimyo Clock Museum
3. Sato Memorial Museum
4. Comic Book & Illustration Museum

5. Yokoyama Memorial Hall
6. Bunkyo Historical Museum
7. Baseball Hall of Fame
8. Century Museum

9. Higuchi Memorial Hall
10. Japan Toy Museum
11. Leather Arts Museum
12. Tokyo National Museum
13. Sogakudo Museum

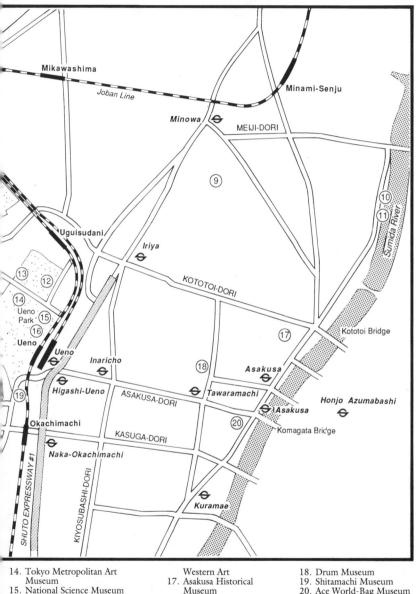

14. Tokyo Metropolitan Art
    Museum
15. National Science Museum
16. National Museum of

Western Art
17. Asakusa Historical
    Museum

18. Drum Museum
19. Shitamachi Museum
20. Ace World-Bag Museum

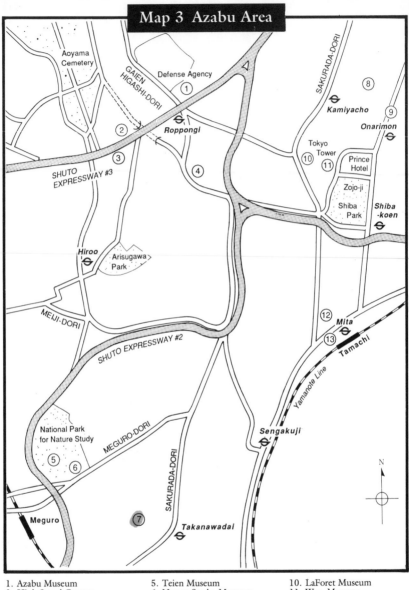

Map 3 Azabu Area

1. Azabu Museum
2. High Speed Camera Museum
3. Pentax Camera Museum
4. Striped House Museum
5. Teien Museum
6. Nature Study Museum
7. Hatakeyama Collection
8. NHK Museum
9. Matsuoka Museum
10. LaForet Museum
11. Wax Museum
12. Minato Ward Museum
13. Industrial Safety Museum

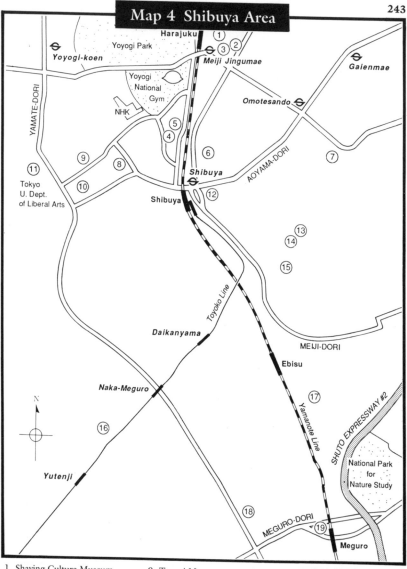

Map 4 Shibuya Area

Harajuku
Yoyogi Park
Yoyogi-koen
Meiji Jingumae
Gaienmae
Yoyogi National Gym
NHK
Omotesando
YAMATE-DORI
Shibuya
AOYAMA-DORI
Shibuya
Tokyo U. Dept. of Liberal Arts
Toyoko Line
Daikanyama
MEIJI-DORI
Ebisu
Naka-Meguro
Yamanote Line
SHUTO EXPRESSWAY #2
N
National Park for Nature Study
Yutenji
MEGURO-DORI
Meguro

1. Shaving Culture Museum
2. Ota Museum
3. Do! Family Art Museum
4. Tobacco & Salt Museum
5. Tepco Museum
6. Children's Hall
7. Nezu Museum
8. Bunkamura Museum
9. Toguri Museum
10. Shoto Museum
11. Tokyo U. Museum of Arts
12. Gotoh Planetarium
13. Shirane Museum
14. Kokugakuin U. Shinto & Archaeology Museums
15. Hanawa Museum
16. Contemporary Sculpture Museum
17. Tokyo Museum of Photography
18. Meguro Museum of Art
19. Kume Museum of Art

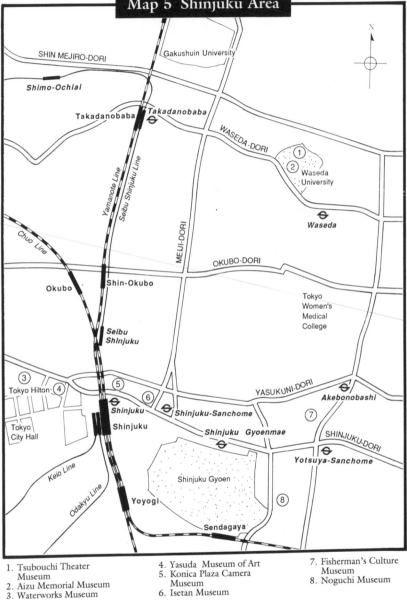

Map 5 Shinjuku Area

N

SHIN MEJIRO-DORI

Gakushuin University

Shimo-Ochiai

Takadanobaba Takadanobaba

WASEDA-DORI

①
②
Waseda University

Yamanote Line

Seibu Shinjuku Line

MEIJI-DORI

Waseda

Chuo Line

OKUBO-DORI

Okubo Shin-Okubo

Tokyo Women's Medical College

Seibu Shinjuku

③
Tokyo Hilton ④

⑤

YASUKUNI-DORI

Akebonobashi

⑥

Shinjuku

Shinjuku-Sanchome

⑦

Shinjuku Shinjuku Gyoenmae

Tokyo City Hall

SHINJUKU-DORI

Keio Line

Yotsuya-Sanchome

Shinjuku Gyoen

Odakyu Line

Yoyogi

⑧

Sendagaya

1. Tsubouchi Theater Museum
2. Aizu Memorial Museum
3. Waterworks Museum

4. Yasuda Museum of Art
5. Konica Plaza Camera Museum
6. Isetan Museum

7. Fisherman's Culture Museum
8. Noguchi Museum

Map 6 Ryogoku, Kinshi Areas

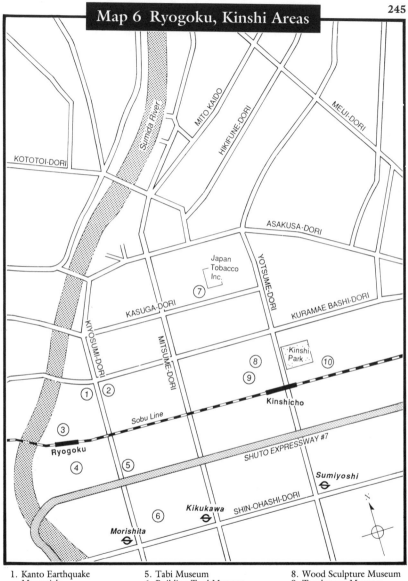

1. Kanto Earthquake
   Memorial
2. Woodcrafts Museum
3. Sumo Museum
4. Sumo Photo. Center

5. Tabi Museum
6. Building Tool Museum
7. Sasaki Gallery

8. Wood Sculpture Museum
9. Tombstone Museum
10. Glass Book Museum